FIX YOUR HOME

TURN YOUR PAD INTO A PALACE

JANE MOSELEY AND JACKIE STRACHAN

PORTICO

CONTENTS

CHAPTER ONE
HOME HELP 6

Fix It Yourself Your own essential toolkit 8

At the Nail Bar Nail ID and hammer hints 10

Learning the Drill Screws, drill types and techniques 12

Fixing It Fixings, tools and techniques 16

Paint Job Paint types and tools 18

Getting the Hang of It Wallpaper types and tools 20

Tile Style Types and tools 22

Getting Stuck In Sealants and adhesives 24

CHAPTER TWO
SMART HOME, SAFE HOME 26

It's All In the Preparation 28

High and Mighty Painting walls and ceilings 32

Wall-to-wall Style Hanging wallpaper 34

Wooden It Be Nice? Painting wooden surfaces 38

The Tile File Preparing, cutting and tiling 42

Take the Floor Flooring types, carpeting and sanding 48

Pack It In Flatpacks 56

Keep It Clean Regular cleaning and the big spring clean 58

Stamp On the Damp, Lick the Limescale Damp, condensation and ventilation 60

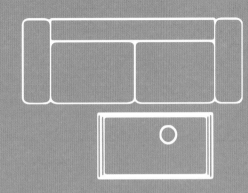

CHAPTER THREE
STYLE ON A SHOESTRING 62

In the Mood Making mood boards 64

Colour It In Loud vs quiet colours and how to use them 66

Your Four Walls Types of wall coverings 70

Light It Up Lighting types and positioning 72

Jazz It Up Types of window treatments 74

Big It Up Space savers, creators and invaders 78

Fill It In Arranging accessories, books and collections 80

Hang It All Hanging pictures and photos 82

Put It Up Shelves and shelving 84

Stash It Storage solutions 86

Home Office Job Designing your home office/work space 90

Swap It, Paint It, Stick It Ideas for upcycling 94

CHAPTER FOUR
SAFE HOME, GREEN HOME 96

Under Lock and Key Locks for doors and windows 98

Keeping An Eye On Things 21st century security 100

Sound the Alarms Smoke and carbon monoxide alarms 102

Don't Lose It Saving water and energy 106

Not Gone With the Wind Insulating and draughtproofing 108

STOCKISTS AND ACKNOWLEDGEMENTS 111

INTRODUCTION

Congratulations and welcome to your new home! You have flown the nest and landed within your own four walls. 'Yay, I've done it' may be followed by 'Eek, now what do I do?'

There's no need to panic. You are in the right place, in every sense. All you need to do is to read this book, paying careful attention to the techniques and practical advice in the first two chapters (Home Help and Smart Home, Safe Home, and then be inspired by ideas on how to

decorate, furnish, accessorize, store and tidy in the Style on a Shoestring section.

There are some useful tips on cleaning, too. Discover which bit does what in your toolkit and how to fix things yourself so that you can save money while transforming your new home.

Get the hang of wallpaper, file tiling in the 'I can do that' box, brush up on painting techniques, learn shelving by the book and get the look you want – all without the bills you don't. Be savvy at storage, a space saver, home office organizer and style maker. Now is your chance to choose the colours that you want, to allow your personality to express itself and to be as minimalist or eclectic as you like.

Use your imagination rather than your income to get a whole new look. There is no need to rush out and spend lots of money on new furniture and curtains; you can repurpose, recycle and reclaim. Check out the final chapter (Safe Home, Green Home) for information on staying safe and being eco-savvy.

So, make like a pro and go from pad to palace without breaking the bank. Let the transformation begin...

CHAPTER ONE
HOME HELP

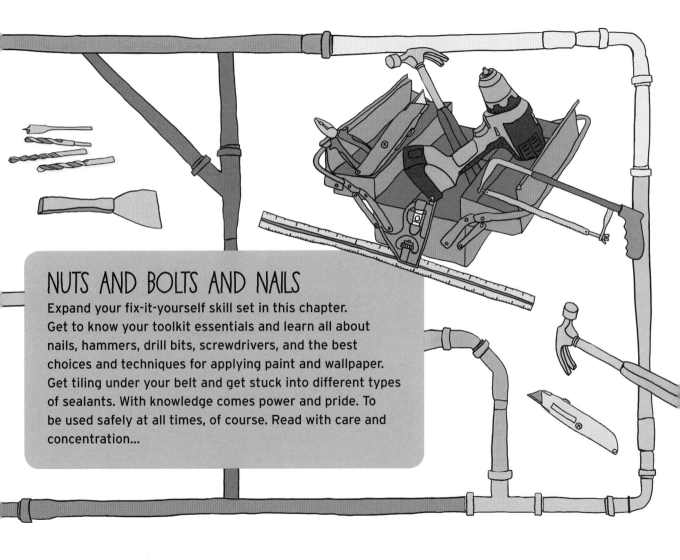

NUTS AND BOLTS AND NAILS

Expand your fix-it-yourself skill set in this chapter.
Get to know your toolkit essentials and learn all about
nails, hammers, drill bits, screwdrivers, and the best
choices and techniques for applying paint and wallpaper.
Get tiling under your belt and get stuck into different types
of sealants. With knowledge comes power and pride. To
be used safely at all times, of course. Read with care and
concentration...

FIX IT YOURSELF

The first step on the rewarding road to fixing your own home is to get properly tooled up. 'Bad workmen blame their tools' is an old saying but a true one. Invest in good-quality tools and keep them safe and clean, preferably in a sturdy tool box, and in one place. Know where and what your tools are: they will become your friends.

THE ESSENTIAL TOOL KIT

There is no need to go overboard and buy every tool in town – this list should suffice as a starting point. Head to your local hardware store and seek advice, have a look at catalogues and research online. Pre-loved is fine, as long as you check they are in good working order. Borrowing tools is tricky and can lead to arguments, so it's much better to have your own to hand at all times.

FLAT-HEAD SCREWDRIVER
For screwing in screws, of course.

BRADAWL
For marking the fixing point for a screw or nail and easing insertion.

CROSS-HEAD SCREWDRIVER
AKA Phillips screwdriver.

ADJUSTABLE SPANNER/WRENCH with a comfortable handle.

MEASURE FOR MEASURE

When drilling holes, cutting tiles or fixing things in place, take time to measure. And always measure twice. Jot down measurements or put them into your smartphone so you have them to hand at the store.

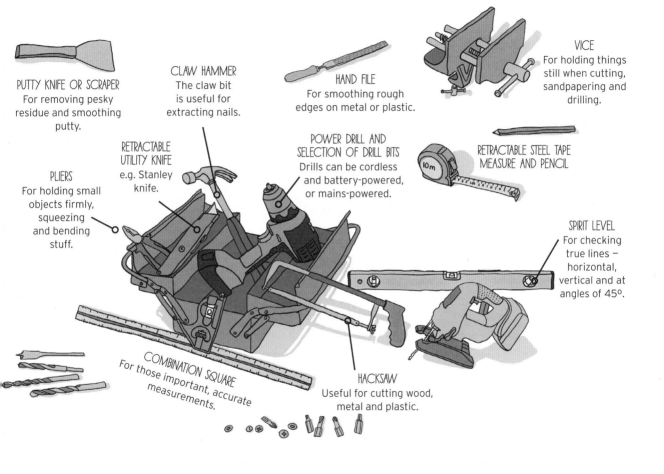

PUTTY KNIFE OR SCRAPER
For removing pesky residue and smoothing putty.

CLAW HAMMER
The claw bit is useful for extracting nails.

HAND FILE
For smoothing rough edges on metal or plastic.

VICE
For holding things still when cutting, sandpapering and drilling.

RETRACTABLE UTILITY KNIFE
e.g. Stanley knife.

POWER DRILL AND SELECTION OF DRILL BITS
Drills can be cordless and battery-powered, or mains-powered.

RETRACTABLE STEEL TAPE MEASURE AND PENCIL

PLIERS
For holding small objects firmly, squeezing and bending stuff.

SPIRIT LEVEL
For checking true lines – horizontal, vertical and at angles of 45°.

COMBINATION SQUARE
For those important, accurate measurements.

HACKSAW
Useful for cutting wood, metal and plastic.

AT THE
NAIL BAR

Nails dating back to ancient times have been found in Egypt – they needed something to keep the coffin lids down on those mummies, after all. Surprisingly, the nail has changed very little since then – in fact, it's a bit of a design classic.

WHICH NAIL?

1 Round wire nail This is a standard metal nail with a head. NB Can split wood. The lost-head version has a smaller head so the nail can be knocked in below the surface in order not to show.
2 Oval wire nail The small head can be knocked in right below the surface; less likely to split wood due to its shape.
3 Tack Short with a wide head, useful for attaching materials such as fabric to wood as the head doesn't disappear into the fabric.
4 Upholstery nail Also short with a wide, rounded, decorative head, to attach fabric to furniture.
5 Masonry nail Made of hardened steel to fix wood to brick, concrete, etc.

HAMMERS

A heavy hammer has more oomph, but you need to be able to lift it in the first place so a mid-size claw hammer is a good compromise. If you opt for second-hand, make sure the head is firmly fixed – you don't want it flying off behind you into the TV!

BEST HAMMER PRACTICE
Hammer square on so the nail stays upright and doesn't slant. If the wood is hard, try starting off with a smaller nail. To preserve your fingers, hold the nail with pliers, or push it through a thin piece of card, then hold the card and bash away with the hammer in safety.

Claw hammer Use the claw part for levering out nails.
Cross-pein/peen One side of the head is narrower, to help start off nails by tapping them in lightly.
Wooden mallet Used to tap wooden joints together, or to strike the head of a chisel or anything that might be damaged by a metal hammer. Not for use with nails.

NAIL PUNCH SET

Confusingly, this is a single item: a punch with a pointed tip. Use it to hammer a nail with a small head (an oval wire nail, for example) below the surface without damaging the surrounding wood.

EXTRACTING NAILS
Slide the V-shaped claw of a claw hammer so it points away from you and push the handle back and forth to lever up the nail. Slide a piece of cardboard under the claw to protect the surface. Or use metal pincers or pliers – grip, wiggle and pull.

LEARNING THE DRILL

A screw is one up on a nail in sophistication. The principle has been around since the year dot, thanks to Archimedes. There's a screw for every occasion, available in all sorts of sizes. Here are a few of the main types.

WHICH SCREW/DRIVER?

Flat-head screw An all-purpose screw for wood (use a flat-head screwdriver, see page 8). Can be countersunk so it doesn't protrude above the surface (unlike a round-head screw).

Cross-head screw The small cross (use a Phillips/cross-head screwdriver, see page 8) makes it harder for the screwdriver to slip out. The Pozidriv screw (a more defined cross) looks similar (needs a Pozidriv screwdriver).

Self-tapping screw Cuts its own thread as it is driven into hard material such as metal or plastic so there's no need to drill a hole first, or you can cut a pilot hole (a smaller hole drilled as a guide).

Ratchet screwdriver and bits The handle moves independently of the screwdriver head. Avoids having to change your grip after each turn. A reverse setting unscrews, or lock it to operate like a normal screwdriver.

TIGHT FIT

If a screw is proving hard to drive in, try putting a little grease on it. If it is proving hard to get out, try screwing it slightly further in first, then unscrew, or spray with penetrating lubricant.

Electric screwdriver and bits The power makes life a lot easier. NB A power drill can also be used as a screwdriver but if you have both, it saves having to change drill bits/screwdriver heads. (See also pages 14–15.)

COUNTERSINKING

Use a countersinking bit on a drill to create a chamfered (sloping) top to the hole you have drilled before inserting a screw. It can then be driven right down so the head is below the surface for a neat finish.

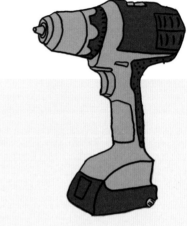

DRILL KIT INSPECTION

Hand drill As Noah would have used on the ark. There's nothing wrong with a humble hand drill, but it's hard work if drilling into something resistant.
Power drill Plenty of power to make light work of hard materials.

To drill through brick or stone, buy one with a hammer action. It's worth investing in a fairly powerful drill with variable speed settings. Use a slow speed (more turning force) for masonry or metal, a higher speed for wood. Buy a set of screwdriver bits and you can use it as a screwdriver, too (see also page 13). Check it has a reverse setting so you can take screws out as well as drive them in.

Fit the drill bit into the chuck (three 'jaws' that open and close) and tighten up (by hand or with a special key) to hold it in place. Make sure the bit is centred and held securely. Different drill bits are available in different sizes for different materials.

DRILL SKILLS

Drilling a hole for a screw makes it easier to drive in and helps to avoid splitting wood. Use a bradawl to make a starter hole (helps prevent the drill skittering across the surface), or make a pilot hole using a drill bit narrower than required. Keep the drill steady and square on to keep the hole straight.

Drill to the depth of the fixing (see page 17). If this is tricky to judge, measure the length of the fixing against the drill bit and stick a small piece of tape onto the bit to mark the length. When drilling a long hole, stop and pull the drill out occasionally to clear out the drilled material.

CORD OR CORDLESS?

Plugging into the electricity source ensures an unlimited supply of power. Cordless gives you the flexibility of working far from a power point, but the rechargeable battery adds weight and won't provide so much power as the mains. It's your call.

Tip If you go cordless, a spare battery is useful for when the first one runs out.

FIXING IT

To hang anything heavier than a photo of your pet on a wall, you will require a secure fixing. But before you get the drill out, you need to know what material you will be drilling into and what might be behind it, so it's time for the tap test.

WHICH WALL?

External walls are normally solid, so fixings will be secure, while internal walls may be of a stud construction – a wood or metal frame lined on either side with plasterboard, which can only support lighter weights. The studs (vertical supports) are usually around 40cm/15¾in apart.

Tap along the wall with your knuckles. Hollow walls (plasterboard with a space/cavity behind) sound, well...hollow or dull, while brick/stone makes a sharper sound (and may hurt). On a hollow wall, listen for a change in the sound from hollow (plasterboard + cavity) to sharper (plasterboard + stud).

SAFETY FIRST

Before drilling into a wall check for hidden water pipes (to avoid a flood) and electric cables (to avoid an electric shock and short circuit), particularly near an electrical fitting. A reliable multipurpose detector is a good investment and should normally detect studs, too. Or turn off the electricity at the consumer unit to protect yourself from shock and use a cordless drill, though this won't avoid the fallout if you do hit a cable or water pipe. (See Drill Skills, page 15.)

PLUG IT

Screws are not normally inserted directly into walls but are screwed into plastic wall plugs, which are tapped into a hole drilled in the wall. As you insert the screw, the plug expands to grip the sides of the hole. Choose the right plug and screw for the wall being drilled, and the weight the fixing must take. If unsure, seek advice. Drill a hole to fit the length and width of the plug, tap in the plug with a hammer and insert the screw.

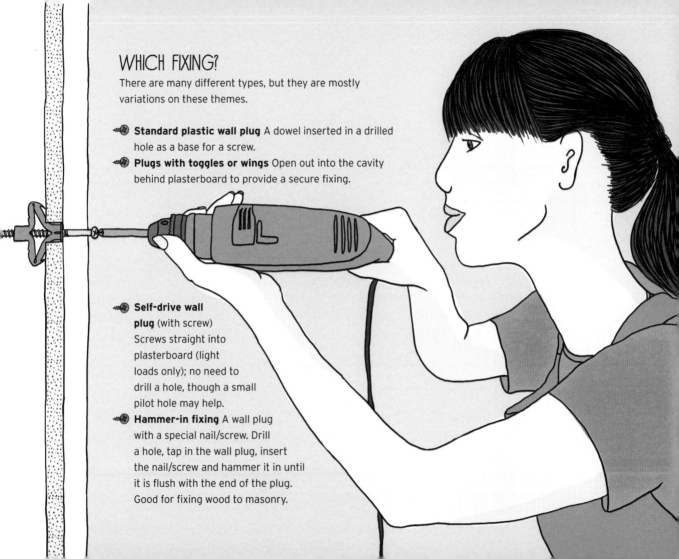

WHICH FIXING?

There are many different types, but they are mostly
variations on these themes.

- **Standard plastic wall plug** A dowel inserted in a drilled
  hole as a base for a screw.
- **Plugs with toggles or wings** Open out into the cavity
  behind plasterboard to provide a secure fixing.

- **Self-drive wall
  plug** (with screw)
  Screws straight into
  plasterboard (light
  loads only); no need to
  drill a hole, though a small
  pilot hole may help.
- **Hammer-in fixing** A wall plug
  with a special nail/screw. Drill
  a hole, tap in the wall plug, insert
  the nail/screw and hammer it in until
  it is flush with the end of the plug.
  Good for fixing wood to masonry.

PAINT JOB

There's a paint for every purpose: you can get special paint for metal radiators, floors, plastic and masonry. And some paints have additional qualities, such as anti-condensation or fire retardant. But here are the paints and finishes most commonly used for ceilings, walls and woodwork.

WHICH PAINT?

Primer Oil- or water-based. Use on new and unpainted surfaces (wood, plaster) to seal the surface and prevent the next coat of paint from sinking in. Check you are using the right primer for the job. Usually followed by, but not to be confused with, an undercoat.

Undercoat Oil- or water-based. A pigmented base that enhances a topcoat. Some paints are sold as not needing an undercoat, but you will usually get a better result with one, and you should definitely use one if you are painting a lighter colour over a darker one.

Gloss Oil- or solvent-based (high odour). Takes several hours to dry. Some water-based, low-odour gloss is now available but the finish is not as durable. Mostly used for woodwork as a topcoat. Wash brushes in white spirit or turpentine.

Emulsion (in one of the first three finishes, see right) Water-based; you may need two coats or to use an undercoat.

Mostly used for walls and ceilings as a topcoat. Low odour. Dries quickly. Wash brushes in warm soapy water.

Acrylic Water-based, more hard-wearing than emulsion. Available in different finishes, so can be used on walls, ceilings and woodwork as a topcoat. Undercoat also available. Low odour. Dries quickly. Wash brushes in warm soapy water.

FINISHES

Matt (flat) Not shiny, helps to hide defects as doesn't reflect light. Marks fairly easily.

Satin (eggshell) Has a sheen so reflects a little more light. Popular for walls and ceilings.

Silk (semi-gloss) Shinier and reflects light. Can be washed so good for bathrooms, kitchens and areas of high traffic. (Special bathroom/kitchen paint is also available.) Can be used for woodwork.

Gloss Very shiny; a good, hard-wearing finish. Normally used for woodwork.

BRUSHES

These come in a range of types and sizes.

Natural bristles Best for oil-based paint.

Synthetic bristles Okay for any paint, but good for water-based paints.

Roller and tray Covers walls and ceilings quickly but watch out for splatters. You'll need a brush to paint around the edges and fiddly bits. Extension poles are available for shorter people painting stuff up high.

Paint pad and tray Produces a smooth finish, easy to use and doesn't splatter like a roller, but you need to load paint more frequently.

See also High and Mighty, page 32; Wooden It Be Nice?, page 38; Eco-paint, page 40.

GETTING THE HANG OF IT

Wallpaper is available in traditional, paste-it-yourself form (a bit messy); or self-adhesive (peel-off backing) and pre-pasted (dip in water) – both are quick but ultimately may not stick as well; or paste-the-wall (easier to cope with fixtures and fittings).

WHICH PAPER?

Standard wallpaper Printed with a design.

Embossed Thick paper embossed with a pattern, usually designed to be painted.

Vinyl/washable Tough, washable and resistant to steam; good for kitchens, bathrooms and areas that get grubby, such as children's rooms. Use a fungicidal paste adhesive. Usually fairly easy to hang and strip (the top may come off to leave the backing, which can serve as a lining paper).

Foil A reflective pattern is picked out in the foil so it is pretty unforgiving on uneven surfaces, where it highlights imperfections. It is often a paste-the-wall type and may need a lining paper.

Flock A design is picked out in a velvet-like pile. Watch for paste staining the flock; vinyl-based flock is more durable and easier to clean.

Lining paper Used to prep walls or ceilings with small imperfections before the decorative paper is applied, or to conceal a dark surface before painting or papering with a lighter colour. Can be hung at right angles to the top paper, i.e. horizontally across a wall, so the joins don't coincide.

GET STUCK IN

Buy a paste to suit the paper you are hanging, e.g. heavy-duty paste for embossed paper, fungicidal paste to help prevent mould forming under non-porous papers (vinyl, washable), stain-free paste for delicate, lightweight paper.

See also Wall-to-wall Style, page 34.

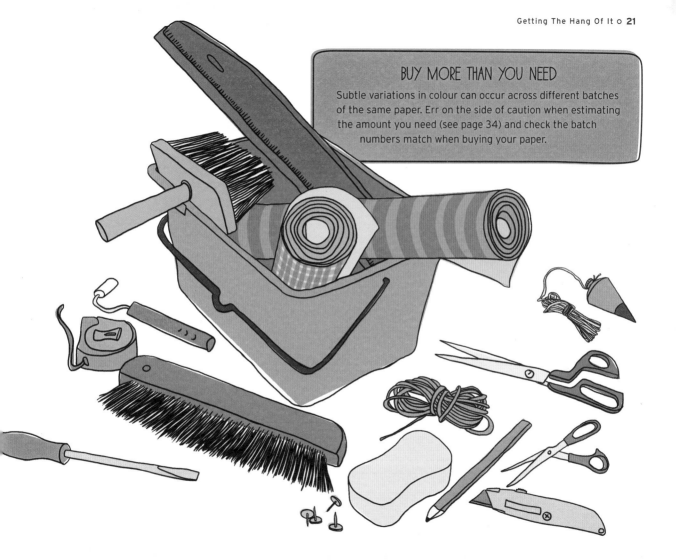

BUY MORE THAN YOU NEED

Subtle variations in colour can occur across different batches of the same paper. Err on the side of caution when estimating the amount you need (see page 34) and check the batch numbers match when buying your paper.

TILE STYLE

The range of tiles for floors and walls might seem a bit bewildering at first, with different finishes available for different locations. When choosing, think about room function, level of traffic and the surface to be tiled, as well as appearance.

WHICH TILE?

Ceramic Hard-wearing and fairly easy to cut, install and maintain; glazed or unglazed.

Porcelain Sounds fragile – aren't antique tea services made of porcelain? In fact it is tougher and more hard-wearing than ceramic, so is often also more expensive. Glazed or unglazed.

Glaze A coating applied to the surface that gives colour and design appeal and makes the tiles resistant to water and staining.

Through-coloured Pigments are added to the tile mixture pre-glazing to match the colour of the glaze surface.

Through-body No glaze or finish – the colour/pattern is consistent.

Glass Difficult to cut, resistant to water but not suitable for most floors as slippery when wet.

Natural stone (marble, granite, slate, travertine, limestone) Trickier to cut but you can buy or hire the equipment, which includes an electric wet saw. If that sounds a bit full-on, you could try a hacksaw with tungsten carbide teeth, or you may prefer to get a professional in. Usually needs sealing and resealing at regular intervals.

Mosaic Small tiles on a mesh backing; often used as a border and to fit around irregular shapes.

TILING TIPS

- Go for the best quality you can afford.
- Check all the tile boxes you buy have the same batch number as the colour can vary, and buy 5–10 per cent extra to cater for wastage/breakages/mistakes.
- Check your supplier will buy back unused boxes if necessary.
- Smaller tiles are easier to cut and fit around fixtures and fittings, and look better.
- A little water can turn a floor – particularly polished glazed tiles – into a small, out-of-season skating rink.
- Porous and unglazed tiles usually need to be treated with a sealant before grouting, to protect against dirt and staining.

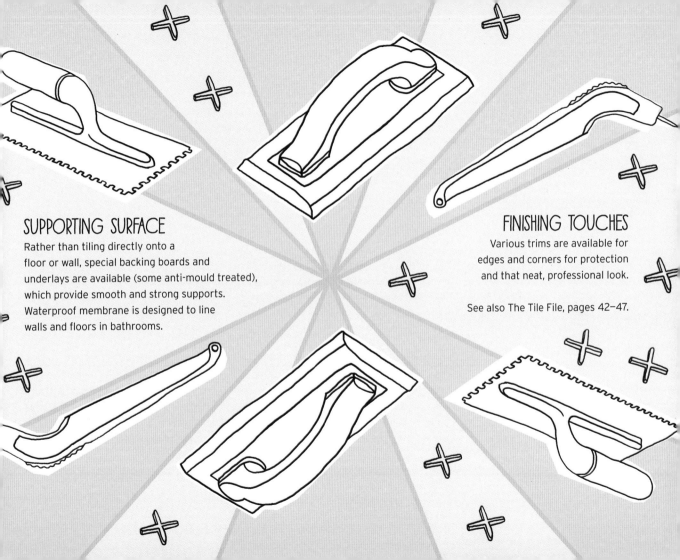

SUPPORTING SURFACE

Rather than tiling directly onto a
floor or wall, special backing boards and
underlays are available (some anti-mould treated),
which provide smooth and strong supports.
Waterproof membrane is designed to line
walls and floors in bathrooms.

FINISHING TOUCHES

Various trims are available for
edges and corners for protection
and that neat, professional look.

See also The Tile File, pages 42–47.

GETTING STUCK IN

Silicone sealant (available in different colours) provides a neat, flexible seal for joints in kitchens and bathrooms. If this is your first time toting a sealant gun, get a little target practice in first on a piece of card to get the feel of it.

You will need

Masking tape
Good quality silicone sealant
Utility knife
Applicator gun
Washing-up liquid
Bowl of water

When sealing a bath or basin, fill it with water first so that when you come to use it, the silicone won't split or come away with the weight.

SEALING THE DEAL

1 Stick masking tape 2mm in from either side of the joint to be sealed if you want a guideline.

2 Make sure the area to be sealed is clean and dry. Cut the nozzle off the sealant tube at an angle of 45º (use a sharp blade for a clean cut) – the point along the nozzle at which you cut controls the amount of silicone that will come out. Cut only a short distance from the end to start; cut off more if you need a larger amount.

3 Using the gun, squeeze the sealant along the joint, as steadily and smoothly as you can.

4 Dip a finger into some washing-up liquid mixed with a little water in a bowl and run it along the silicone, smoothing and pressing in slightly; keep wetting your finger. Remove any tape and leave the silicone to set.

OUT WITH THE OLD ...

To remove old sealant, try prising up
one end with a knife and pulling it away.
You might need to run along the edges
carefully with a knife first. You can also
buy sealant remover, or spray with a
penetrating lubricant, leave for several
minutes and then scrape off.

... AND IN WITH THE NEW

To ensure the new sealant sticks it's
important to remove all traces of the
old – use a toothbrush and white spirit. If
mould or mildew are present, scrub with
a mix of one part bleach to two parts
water (take the necessary precautions
around bleach), then rinse.

CHAPTER TWO
SMART HOME, SAFE HOME

USING YOUR SKILL SET

Now you are something of a DIY maestro, it's time to put your new skills into practice. Learn how to prepare surfaces, how to paint walls and ceilings, the ups and downs of hanging wallpaper, the ins and outs of damp and ventilation. Discover how to unpack the flatpack. Never be floored by floors again and get the low-down on the big clean. Here is everything you need to get your four walls and floors into shape.

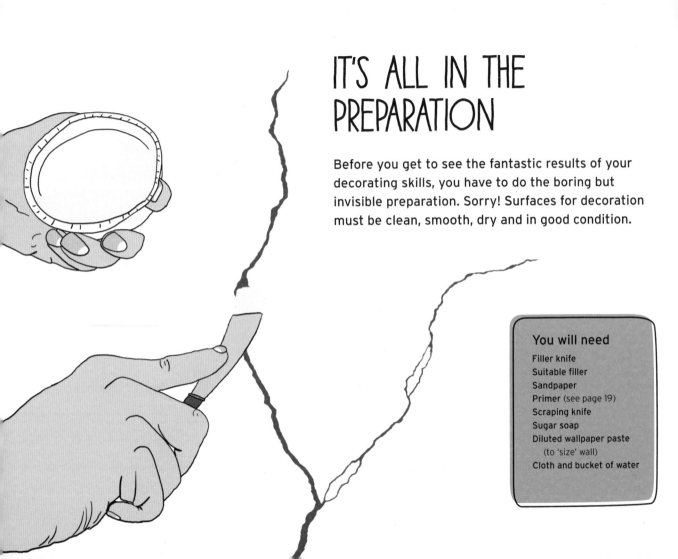

IT'S ALL IN THE PREPARATION

Before you get to see the fantastic results of your decorating skills, you have to do the boring but invisible preparation. Sorry! Surfaces for decoration must be clean, smooth, dry and in good condition.

You will need

Filler knife
Suitable filler
Sandpaper
Primer (see page 19)
Scraping knife
Sugar soap
Diluted wallpaper paste
   (to 'size' wall)
Cloth and bucket of water

SIZE MATTERS

Strictly speaking, if you apply a primer you don't also need sizing, but it does make the paper easier to position and to remove later. Some primers combine both primer and size.

PREPPING FOR PAINT OR TILES

New (dry) or unpainted plaster or plasterboard Apply a coat of primer.

Painted plaster or plasterboard Scrape off flaky old paint, wash down with sugar soap and water, and allow to dry. If painting over gloss paint, sand the wall, brush and wipe with a damp cloth, or apply a bonding primer to provide a key for the new paint.

PREPPING FOR WALLPAPER

New (dry) or unpainted plaster or plasterboard Apply a coat of primer, then 'size' with a coat of wallpaper paste diluted in water as a sealant (see the packet for proportions), or use a proprietary primer/sealer. Size helps to slide the pasted paper into position and makes it easier to remove when you want another new look.

Painted plaster or plasterboard Sand the wall, brush down and wipe with a damp cloth. Size the wall as above.

Gloss paint Wash the wall, allow to dry, sand lightly, brush down and wipe with a damp cloth, then size the wall as above.

Emulsion paint Hold a damp cloth against a painted area for about 30 seconds, and then rub the wall with it. If only a little paint comes off proceed as for gloss paint, then size as above. However, if a lot comes off, wash the wall thoroughly with sugar soap and water (or even sand and wash it to remove as much paint as you can – not a quick job!), then size as above.

FILLING

1 To fill small holes and cracks with a suitable filler, rake out any loose material and brush off the dust. Press in the filler with a flexible knife, smooth off the excess, allow to dry and sand smooth.

2 If the filler shrinks when dry, repeat with more filler.

3 Paint primer over the filled area to prevent the patch showing through when the wall is covered.

STRIPPING WALLPAPER

You will need

Stripping knife
Wallpaper stripper solution (or make your own, see right)
Utility knife or wallpaper scorer
Large sponge or brush
Bucket for water
Plastic bags
Decorators' caulk

1 Removing wallpaper can be very therapeutic when it comes off easily in long strips, but when it sticks to the wall tenaciously like a small dog to a large bone it's a different matter, and you need to douse it in warm water or steam.

2 Try pulling at a corner of the old wallpaper, just in case it decides to come away easily. If not, score the old paper with a utility knife or wallpaper scorer, being careful not to damage the surface underneath. This helps the water or steam to soak in, which will make the job easier.

3 Before you start wetting the wall, tape plastic bags over light fittings and electric sockets, and switch off the electricity at the consumer unit as a safety precaution against water penetration.

4 Fill a bucket with warm water. You can add wallpaper stripper solution, or make your own using fabric conditioner (one part conditioner to two parts water) or vinegar (one part vinegar to three parts water). Using a large sponge or brush, soak the wallpaper, avoiding water penetrating light fittings and electrical

STRIPPING OFF VS PAPERING OVER

It's generally best to remove old wallpaper, though you can paper over it if it's stuck down well. Some wallpapers allow you to peel the top layer off so you can paper on top, treating the backing paper as a lining. Size the paper as described on page 29.

sockets at all costs. Allow the water to soak in for 4–5 minutes.

5 Using a stripping knife, scrape the paper off the wall, working from the bottom upwards. Re-wet the paper as required. Ensure all bits of paper and adhesive are removed and wash down the wall. It's a tedious job but well worth spending time on as the smoother the wall, the better your freshly decorated surfaces will look.

6 Gaps between walls and skirting board can be filled with decorators' caulk.

LET OFF SOME STEAM

Steam strippers can be bought or hired. Score the surface as described and follow the manufacturer's instructions. Wear good gloves and long sleeves to protect against drips of hot water.

See also High and Mighty, pages 32–33; Wall-to-wall Style, pages 34–37; Wooden It Be Nice?, pages 38–41; The Tile File, pages 42–47.

HIGH AND MIGHTY

With surfaces prepared (see pages 28-29) and paint chosen, it's time to don your dungarees and get to work. Start at the top and work down – paint woodwork (see pages 38-41) and ceilings first, then walls, working from the top down.

DON'T DRY OUT

If you need to take a break, wrap your brush in plastic wrap, or rest your brush/roller in the tray and cover the whole thing in wrap.

PAINT PERFECT – WALLS AND CEILINGS

You will need

Screwdriver (to loosen fittings) **Paint** (see page 19)
Stick (to stir paint)
Dust sheets/newspaper (for protection)
Brushes/rollers (see page 19)
Suitable ladder
Cloth

1 For a neat look, switch off the electricity and loosen light fittings first so you don't get paint on them. Paint in daylight whenever you can. Stir paint before using and cover floor in dust sheets or newspaper.

2 On ceilings (best with a roller or pad), start at a window and work away from it.

3 On both ceilings and walls, use a small brush to paint around edges, in corners and around light fittings, feathering out your strokes so they will blend in when you paint the rest. Start at a wall with a window and work away from it. Never leave a whole surface unfinished to be completed the next day – as with a bad wig, you will definitely see the join. Wipe off drips with a cloth as you go before they harden.

4 Work in sections and apply the paint in a series of strokes in random directions. Finish by going across the section again lightly, this time in one direction to even out and smooth the paint.

Ceilings

A brush can be used for the whole ceiling, but you will find you are moving the ladder constantly, so a roller or pad with an extending handle is easier. Work across in strips.

WALL-TO-WALL STYLE

With surfaces prepared (see pages 28–31) and wallpaper selected, you are good to go. For a professional result, switch off the electricity at the consumer unit, and loosen electrical fittings before you start so you can tuck the paper edges underneath.

You will need

Tape measure/steel rule
Plumb line
Screwdriver (to loosen fittings)
Wallpaper paste (to suit your paper)
Bucket
Stick (to stir paste)
Wallpaper (see page 20)
Scissors (long and sharp)
Long pasting table
Pasting brush
Suitable ladder
Paper hanging brush
Clean cloth (to wipe excess paste)
Seam roller

HOW MUCH PAPER?

Ceilings Measure the length and width of the room at its longest and widest points.

Walls Measure the height and add 150mm/6in per length to allow for trimming top and bottom. Take windows and doors into account, but add extra if the paper contains a pattern (around 15 per cent per length for a large repeat pattern – the roll label may offer guidance).

Check the length and width of the roll of your chosen paper and work out how many rolls you need. Back up your estimate using an online calculator if you are not sure. Check the label of your chosen wallpaper to see if a lining paper is required.

STRAIGHT LINES

It is important to hang paper straight so visiting friends won't think they have blundered into the House of Fun at the end of the pier by mistake. Hang a plumb line around 25mm/1in in from the corner of the first wall and fix it at the top with a drawing pin. Carefully mark its position on the wall at intervals down the line. Then using a straight edge or long spirit level, draw along the marks to make a straight vertical line.

For a feature (single) wall or a chimney breast you will get the best effect by centring the first length of paper in the width of the wall and then working outwards to either side.

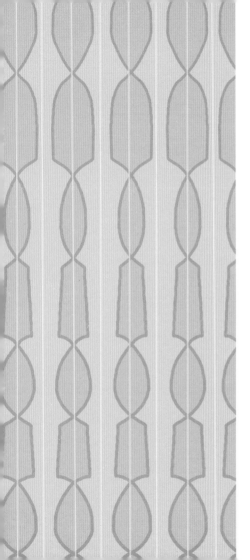

CUTTING AND PASTING

1 In a bucket mix the paste to suit your wallpaper (see packet). Cut a length, including extra for the trim. If the paper has a repeat pattern, add extra to subsequent lengths to allow for this – check the roll label for guidance.

2 Lay the paper on the table, reverse side up, and brush on the paste, working from the centre outwards. Paste evenly and right to the edges. When one half of the length is covered, without creasing, loosely fold it in half back onto itself to the middle, so the pasted side sticks together. Repeat with the second half. Leave for 2–3 minutes (or as instructed on the packet) so that the paper absorbs the paste.

3 Hang the pasted paper over an arm to climb the ladder. Unfold the top part and hold it against the top of the wall (pattern the right way up), leaving around 75mm/3in overlap onto the ceiling. Align the edge of the paper against the vertical line you have drawn (see page 35). Using the dry paper hanging brush, brush down across the paper, working from the centre out to each side, unfolding the paper as you go. If you need to reposition it, pull the paper away carefully.

4 With the back of the scissors, score a crease where the paper meets the ceiling and skirting board, pull the paper away slightly, cut along the crease and brush back into place. Wipe off excess paste from the ceiling or skirting board before it dries. Hang the next length so it butts up neatly against the first, matching any pattern, and continue around the room. Wipe off excess paste at the seams and use a seam roller to press them down.

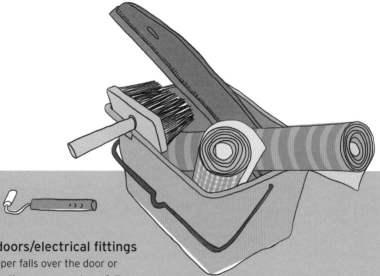

Corners

Trim the paper to leave a strip around 25mm/1in in width to fold around the corner. Gently push the paper into or around the corner with your fingers and brush it down (make small cuts in the trim top and bottom as required). Paste the next sheet so it overlaps the strip for a neat finish. Before you do, check the vertical with the plumb line in case the corner has thrown it out and mark it on the paper lightly – corners are notoriously unreliable.

Windows/doors/electrical fittings

Where the paper falls over the door or fitting, feel for the corners and carefully cut the paper diagonally into them. Fold back the excess, score creases with the back of the scissors, pull the paper away and cut along the crease. If the fitting has been loosened and the electricity has been turned off at the consumer unit, push the edges in under the fitting – the amount you tuck in should only be small, not touching the fitting interior. Allow the paper to dry before refastening the fitting.

Ceilings

A candidate for that hilarious home video moment. As you paste the paper, fold it in short, concertina-style folds. Supporting the paper with one hand, unfold the first part and position it against the ceiling. Ideally, have a lovely assistant to hold the paper up behind you while you use both hands to apply it and brush it into place.

WOODEN IT BE NICE?

A lick of paint on woodwork soon freshens up a room, but it's worth taking time with the topcoat, which will betray the way it was applied: either smoothly like a TV makeover pro, or a bit slapdash with your phone tucked under your chin.

PREPPING WOOD FOR PAINT

Bare new wood Sand down rough areas with fine sandpaper. Treat knots with a sealant to stop resin seeping through. Use masking tape or paint shield as necessary. Apply a coat of primer and allow to dry, then an undercoat, followed by a topcoat. If you apply a second topcoat of gloss, sand the first down lightly and wipe with a damp cloth.

Painted wood Wash down with sugar soap and water. If the old paint is gloss, sand down with fine sandpaper (and wipe with a damp cloth) to provide a key for the new paint. Remove flaking paint with a scraper. Fill dips, cracks or small holes with a suitable filler, allow to dry and sand smooth. Apply a sealant to any knots weeping resin. Apply an undercoat, then a topcoat. You might get away with just sanding down and applying a topcoat; it depends on the colour and condition of the paint underneath. Fill gaps between the skirting board and wall with decorator's caulk.

You will need

Fine sandpaper
Knot sealant
Masking tape/paint shield
Paint (see page 19)
Brushes/rollers (see page 19)
Cloth
Sugar soap
Bucket
Scraper
Filling knife
Suitable filler
Dust sheets/newspaper (for protection)
Stick to stir paint
Decorators' caulk
Old jar/tin (to clean brushes)
White spirit/turpentine and rag

PAINT PERFECT - WOOD

Protect surfaces and furniture. To protect glass, stick masking tape on parts adjacent to the wood. To paint around door handles etc., loosen them first, or protect with masking tape providing it won't react with any lacquered coating. Otherwise, just be very careful and use a small brush!

Paint those parts of doors and windows that open/close early in the day to allow time to dry. Wipe up drips and spills as you go. Apply the paint with smooth strokes in the direction of the wood grain. For broad areas, apply strokes both across and with the grain, followed by smooth strokes in the direction of the grain. Finish by applying the tip of the brush in one long stroke to smooth out the paint, lifting it off the surface gently so as not to leave a mark. Protect the wall above the skirting board by holding a piece of card against it with one hand while you wield the brush with the other.

ECO-PAINT

The solvents used in paint give off VOCs (volatile organic compounds), hence their odour – even for several years after their application, which can cause irritation and respiratory problems. Natural eco-paints are available, some more 'solvent-free' than others, so check the labels before buying.

WHICH WOOD?

Real wood Expensive but looks good. It can be worked easily and painted, but may contain knots (not knuts!) and may warp. When buying a length, hold it up to one eye and look down it to check for warping.

Chipboard Chips of wood are held together with resin. The surface is coarse but is often finished with a thin melamine surface with a 'wood look'. Strong and cheaper than wood, it is often used for the carcass of kitchen units and worktops. Swells if it absorbs moisture, and can chip or flake.

MDF (medium-density fibreboard) Mashed-up wood fibres held together with resin. The finish is smoother than chipboard and so is easy to paint; it is often used to make cabinets and cupboards. Swells if it absorbs moisture.

Plywood Thin layers of wood veneer glued together. Quite light and very strong, good resistance to warping; often used for panelling and flooring.

STORING PAINT

To prevent a skin developing on the top of the paint when you store it, close the lid firmly, then turn the pot upside down for a few seconds to seal it with paint. (But store the right way up of course!)

THE TILE FILE

Tiling mistakes are expensive and tricky to correct, so the golden rule is measure, check and measure again. Note the manufacturer's drying times. As a rule wait 24 hours before grouting, and two days before using a shower/ bath area.

You will need

Protective glasses
Cold chisel
Hammer
Spacers (to suit tile size; available in different widths, they dictate the size of the grout gap and ensure it is uniform)
Tape measure
Pencil
Spirit level/plumb line
Wooden batten
Tiles (see page 22)
Notched trowel
Suitable adhesive
Sponge and bucket of water
Suitable grout
Grout float

PREPPING WALLS

1 If you need to remove old tiles, protect the floor using dustsheets or newspaper and yourself by wearing goggles. Starting at the edge of a wall, position a cold chisel between the wall and a tile, tap with a hammer and the tiles should start coming away.

2 Chisel off the remains of any adhesive. The surface to be tiled must be smooth and dry (see page 29). You can also tile on a backing board (see page 23).

3 Make a tile gauge by laying several tiles separated by spacers along a straight length of wood (a batten) and carefully marking their positions on it.

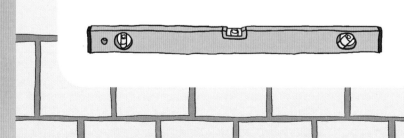

START POINT (STRAIGHT/BRICK LAYOUT)

If possible, tile from the centre of the wall widthways, working out to either side, and from the bottom to top. Begin by fixing your start point. Don't start from a corner or the skirting board as they probably won't be dead straight and will throw everything out. Measure and mark the centre of the wall with a cross (measure the height from the top of the skirting board). Working down the wall from the centre, use the tile gauge to see how deep the bottom tile will be. If less than half a tile, raise the central point slightly. Now mark down the wall from the revised central point to show where each row of tiles will fall.

Repeat the measuring/adjusting process across the width of the wall – ideally the tiles at either end will not be too narrow. Use a spirit level (or plumb line, see page 35) to draw a vertical line down the wall across the (new) central point. Then draw a horizontal line across the wall where the base of the bottom row of **whole** tiles will fall. Nail/screw a temporary wooden batten just below this base line (avoiding cables/pipes, see page 16) for the first row of tiles (check the batten with a spirit level). Mark the centre of the wall widthways on the batten. Place your first tile so the base rests on the batten with one side of the tile a little to one side of the centre mark (to allow for the grout space).

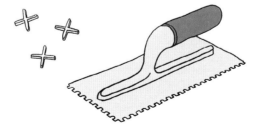

TILING

Using a notched trowel, spread adhesive evenly over the wall, a small section at a time, as it dries quickly. Place the first tile on the wall at your start point (see page 43) – use a spirit level to check it vertically and horizontally, and continue placing tiles, inserting spacers between them as you go. Press each tile into the adhesive, wiggling it slightly so it beds down well. Insert the spacers so they stand out and can be removed from the wall before the adhesive dries. Don't apply adhesive around the perimeter until you are ready to apply the edge tiles. Using a damp sponge, lightly wipe off any excess adhesive from the tiles as you work. (See Cutting Tiles, page 46.)

GROUTING

When the tiles are dry, mix the grout following the manufacturer's instructions. Using a grout float, spread the grout between the tiles, working it in well – you might need to use your fingers in corners. Leave for a few minutes, then wipe over the tiles with a damp sponge to remove the excess grout, keeping it flat so you don't dig out the grout (have a bucket of water handy to rinse out the sponge regularly).

To clean old white grout

Use a toothbrush and scrub with a paste of baking soda and a little water, or baking soda, vinegar and water. For mould and mildew, try the bleach and water mix on page 61. Special grout cleaners are also available. Don't use bleach on coloured grout.

If that doesn't work

Work a grout rake or scraper up and down to remove the old grout to a depth of around 3mm/⅛in; angle the rake to make sure you remove it in the width of the joint too. Clean with a toothbrush to remove all dust and go over with a vacuum if possible, then apply new grouting (see left).

DON'T BE STUCK UP

Try to avoid washing grout or tile adhesive down a drain or sink as it will harden and block it up. Wear thin vinyl gloves since adhesive can be a nightmare to get off if it hardens on hands and nails.

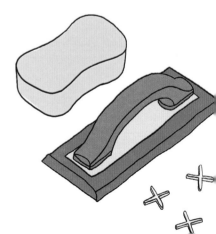

Leave a 3mm/$\frac{1}{8}$in gap between the bottom row of tiles and the bath or basin to allow room for the sealant (see page 24).

CUTTING TILES

Straight cut

Use a tile scorer and straight edge to score a line on the tile along which to cut. Place the tile on a piece of wood (or work surface) so that the scored line aligns with one edge of the wood, press down on the unsupported side and the tile should snap along the line. Make sure the complete length of the file is scored evenly, including ends, or it will not snap cleanly. Or use a flat-bed tile cutter. (Specialist cutters are needed for certain tiles.)

Edge tiles

To cut to the correct size, place a tile over the last whole tile in a row, butting up squarely against the edge of the wall. Mark off the amount you need, allowing for the grout gap, and draw a line for scoring.

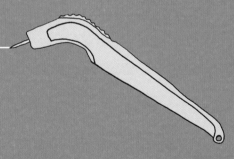

SAFETY FIRST

If you have to tile around an electrical fitting/socket,
always switch off the electricity at the consumer unit, as
wet hands and electricity are extremely dangerous.

LAYOUTS

Tiles can be laid out in various patterns, from straight (all aligning with each other), to diagonal (creating a diamond pattern) and brick/offset (each row is staggered above the other).

Odd shapes

Score the tile as required (a shape tracer can be used to make a template for awkward shapes) and use the nipper to snip away at the tile, small bits at a time. Or you can use a tile saw or a ceramic cutting blade on a jigsaw. Wear protective glasses as shards of tile can be as sharp as glass.

TAKE THE FLOOR

When choosing a type of flooring, as well as appearance, don't forget to take into account the amount of traffic (as in people, pets, toy cars...) the room can expect, how you want it to feel under foot and any noise issues.

OH SO QUIET

Carpet is the best flooring for noise reduction, while hard floors are at the opposite end of the scale but good for tap dancing practice. If you want to install a hard floor while still keeping noise down, look at using a special underlay or a 'floating floor' – check out the advice at your DIY store.

WHICH FLOOR?

Solid wood The natural wood of floorboards can come up a treat when sanded, and stained or varnished (see page 50).

Laminate MDF printed with a wood-effect finish. Knocks and chips easily. Can be DIY fitted (see pages 54–55).

Engineered wood A real wood veneer is applied to a base. Can be DIY-fitted.

Bamboo A sustainable, fast-growing, natural grass rather than a wood, although similar in appearance to wood when used as flooring. Slightly more resistant to water damage and warping than wood. The adhesive used to compress the layers together can release VOCs (see page 40). Tends to scratch.

Ceramic/porcelain/natural stone tiles (see page 52). Cold under bare feet, easy to clean, hard-wearing and usually resistant to water.

Vinyl Available in sheets, or tiles and planks that are easy to fit (see page 52). Often printed with a pattern or effect (e.g. stone or wood) and sometimes textured. Not really recyclable.

Lino (linoleum) Available in sheets and tiles. Very durable and eco-friendly, lino has been around since the 19th century, but in its modern form is biodegradable. Normally requires protecting with an acrylic sealer, and re-sealing at intervals.

Water-resistant but not waterproof. It doesn't harbour bacteria or dust mites and so is good for allergy sufferers.

Rubber Available in sheets and tiles. Can be a bit industrial-looking but resilient and comes in different colours and textures.

Seagrass A natural fibre in natural colours woven into matting, a bit harsh under bare feet. Other natural fibres include coir, jute and sisal.

Carpet Available on rolls and in tiles. Warm underfoot and helps keep heat in.

SANDING AND STAINING FLOORBOARDS

Providing the local woodworm haven't been dining out on it, a real wooden floor looks great with only a little smartening up. But if opting for the natural look on anything other than a small area, it's best to hire a sanding machine.

You will need

Sander
Hammer
Sandpaper
Wood filler
Filling knife
Gloves
Respiratory mask
Cloth

1 Huge amounts of dust will be created, so the room needs to be empty. Do any wall decorating first, unless applying a textured surface that dust might adhere to.

2 Tap down protruding nails below the surface. Check for and treat any woodworm. Keep internal doors and windows closed and wear a suitable respiratory mask.

3 Starting in a corner, work across the room diagonally in overlapping strips. If necessary, repeat in the opposite diagonal direction, but follow the direction of the boards for your last pass.

4 Sand corners and awkward bits by hand, but an edge sander can do the perimeter.

5 Vacuum the floor and wipe with a damp cloth.

6 Leave the room for a day to allow the dust to settle, vacuum and wipe again.

WHAT FINISH?

Stain Colours but doesn't protect wood, so is normally followed by a coat of oil or varnish. Two coats are usually needed for a good depth of colour. Sand lightly in the direction of the grain between coats.

Varnish Provides a hard-wearing surface. Usually solvent-based so wear a respiratory mask. Two or three coats are normally needed, particularly if applying over stain. Sand lightly between coats in the direction of the grain.

Oil/wax Not super durable so needs to be reapplied every couple of years. Remove excess oil with a clean cloth to avoid a patchy finish. Repeat with additional coats as necessary. When dry, buff the wood using a cloth.

Paint Once down it is pretty much for keeps as it is very hard to remove. Use an appropriate paint with a coat of primer first. You will probably need at least two coats and you may need to sand lightly between them.

Wear gloves and a respiratory mask if necessary and ensure the room is ventilated. Start at the furthest point from the door and reverse your way out as you work, as if leaving the royal presence.

Fill gaps between floorboards (see page 110) and small holes and cracks with wood filler. Allow to dry and sand the filled areas by hand.

LAYING FLOOR TILES

The floor must be firm, dry and flat. Apply a suitable primer to porous surfaces such as plywood, chipboard and cement. Check with your supplier to see if you need an underlay or membrane, or if you want to tile over an existing covering.

You will need

Tiles (carpet, ceramic/stone or vinyl)
Suitable adhesive
Utility knife
Low-tack adhesive or carpet tape
 (some tiles have self-adhesive backing)

Notched adhesive spreader
Straight edge/steel rule
Tape measure
Pencil

1 Measure and mark a cross in the centre of the room – you'll get the best effect by starting here. Double-check that the lines of the cross are parallel with the sides of the room, so the tiles will be laid straight.

2 Loose lay (no adhesive) a test row of tiles across the full width and length of the room. If the tiles at the edges will be too narrow and therefore hard to cut, adjust your start point as necessary.

VINYL TILES

3 Follow steps 1 and 2. Use a utility knife to cut the tiles, or score right across them with a knife and then bend until they snap.

4 Apply the adhesive with a notched spreader. Spread enough to lay around 1 sq. m/10¾ sq. ft at a time. Butt the edges together tightly and press them down (a rolling pin is useful).

5 Wipe off excess adhesive as you go with a damp cloth.

CARPET TILES

3 Follow steps 1 and 2. Use low-tack adhesive or double-sided carpet tape so the tiles can be removed/replaced easily. Score and cut tiles on the reverse side.

4 Arrows on the back indicate the direction of the pile – lay them all the same way or alternately for a chequerboard effect.

CERAMIC OR STONE TILES

3 Follow steps 1 and 2, or fasten a temporary wooden batten at the perimeter for a row of whole tiles and work from that.

4 See pages 42–47 for applying tiles and grouting.

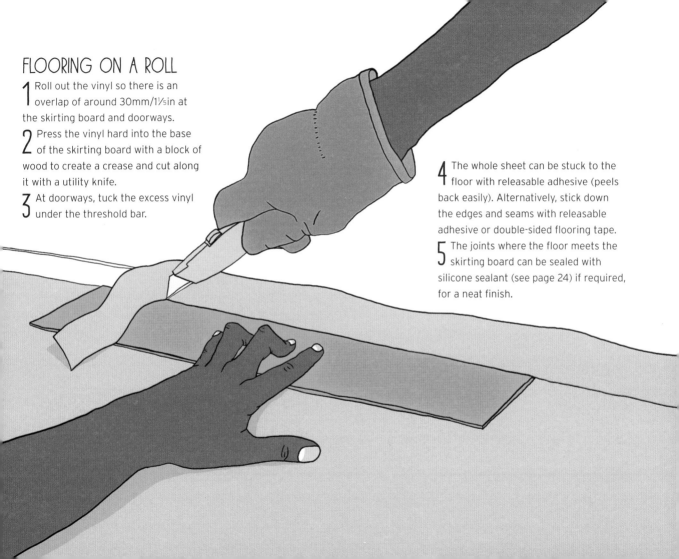

FLOORING ON A ROLL

1 Roll out the vinyl so there is an overlap of around 30mm/1⅕in at the skirting board and doorways.

2 Press the vinyl hard into the base of the skirting board with a block of wood to create a crease and cut along it with a utility knife.

3 At doorways, tuck the excess vinyl under the threshold bar.

4 The whole sheet can be stuck to the floor with releasable adhesive (peels back easily). Alternatively, stick down the edges and seams with releasable adhesive or double-sided flooring tape.

5 The joints where the floor meets the skirting board can be sealed with silicone sealant (see page 24) if required, for a neat finish.

LAYING LAMINATE

Laminate can be laid over most floors (timber, concrete, vinyl, ceramic tiles, etc.) as long as they are dry and flat and you have a suitable underlay (and damp-proof membrane, if required). Check out the options at your DIY store.

You will need

Laminate, trim, threshold strips
Expansion spacers (allow for natural movement)
Steel rule
Hacksaw or jigsaw
Suitable adhesive

1 Before you buy, think about the direction that you want to lay the laminate. Boards laid lengthways in a long room accentuate the length, but laid widthways the effect is to add width. Buy extra for wastage. Leave the laminate in the room in which it is to be laid for 48 hours so it acclimatizes to the conditions.

2 Once the underlay and any damp-proof membrane is fitted, loose-lay a length of boards, end to end, the complete length of the room, to check how long the last board will be. If less than a third of its length, shorten the first board so neither of the end boards will be too short. Loose-lay the boards across the room width, to make sure the boards at the perimeter are not too narrow and therefore hard to cut and fit.

3 Place the first board (cut to fit as required) in a corner with spacers at the top and the side. Fit the next board end to end – slot it in at a 30° angle and lower to click into place. Continue down the length of the room and cut the end board to fit. If the offcut is over

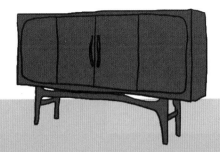

300mm/12in use it to start the next length. If not, cut another board in half. Place the cut end of the next board against the wall, with a spacer, and slot/click into position next to the first board. The joints (ends of the boards) should not line up but should be staggered so they are around a minimum of 150mm/6in apart.

4 When the floor is finished, remove the spacers and cover the gaps with trim – glued to the skirting board not the floor. Mitre the corners for a neat look. Threshold strips ensure a neat transition from the laminate to the adjacent flooring and pipe-hole covers neaten the fit around radiator pipes. Cut out a plug of board so it can be slid either side of the pipe, shorten the plug to accommodate the pipe, then replace it. Use a shape tracer to cut around awkward shapes.

HOW TO CUT BOARDS

Cut boards with a fine-toothed hacksaw or jigsaw (right side up).

PACK IT IN

Do not fear the flatpack. There are a few dos and don'ts when it comes to flatpack etiquette but if you keep a close eye on these, on the instructions that come with the kit and on the parts, large and small, you will avoid potential pitfalls, frustration and fails.

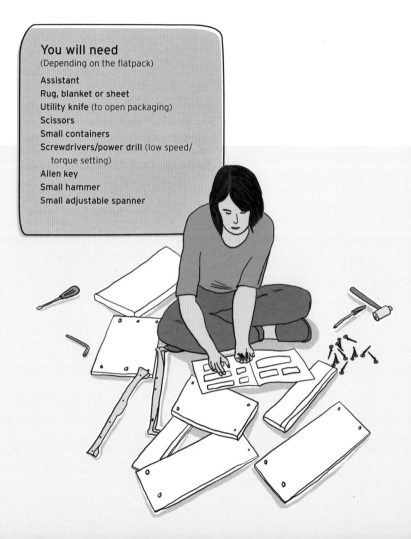

You will need
(Depending on the flatpack)

Assistant
Rug, blanket or sheet
Utility knife (to open packaging)
Scissors
Small containers
Screwdrivers/power drill (low speed/ torque setting)
Allen key
Small hammer
Small adjustable spanner

Unpacking Unpack your item in the room it will call home. If it is particularly large (e.g. a wardrobe) or complex, or if the leaflet specifically states this is a two-person job, enlist or bribe a friend/family member to hold things for you, decipher the instructions or take on the more technical parts.

Protecting Use an old sheet or rug (or the flatpack packaging itself) to prevent damage to any parts or the floor. Things might get a bit dusty so dress down. Give yourself time and space. Don't try and build a bookshelf before breakfast in your best bib and tucker in a busy bedroom. Bad timing = bad time.

Checking Don't skip the dull but necessary stage of counting and checking off all the parts: identify each screw, nail, bolt, nut, tack and hinge. Use small containers to keep the different fixings apart, particularly the different-sized screws. Using the wrong one could ruin everything.

Inspecting Look for any damage in transit. You can then decide if you need to take the item back.

Be tool-ready Have your tools to hand, including a power drill and maybe a power screwdriver, fully charged. Some kits come with their own tools, but you may find using your own easier and more effective. Similarly, you might find your own hexagonal Allen key more useful than the one supplied.

Read the instructions Study from beginning to end! A quick flick and speed read does not cut it. Then follow them. Someone with the required know-how has written them, and now is not the time to go your own way.

Divide and separate Divide the various elements into logical groups: base, sides, doors, legs, shelves, wheels, etc.

Don't get stuck The base and sides are usually assembled first, using the ready-made holes and fixings. If glue is involved, don't go overboard or over the carpet. Wait a day for it to dry thoroughly before using your flatpack item.

Final checks Finish the fittings and fixings by hand rather than with the power drill, or use the latter but on a low setting only. Check everything is in its place and tighten any hinges only when you have checked the doors are straight.

KEEP IT CLEAN

Spring-cleaning keeps your home hygienic and safe, and it makes you feel better (promise). It is a rite of spring and the right spring thing to do. It's not a quick dust-and-done, wipe-and-walk affair – you need to schedule and dedicate a few days to do it properly. But there are ways of making the process – the journey to safe, sound and sparkly – more manageable, even enjoyable. Divide it into chunks. Take a room a day, a task at a time. Write a checklist and tick off tasks as you complete them. There is nothing more satisfying than a ticked-off to-do list. Rewards at the end of various stages also help motivate you (these can involve long baths, chocolate, a glass of wine).

SORT OUT YOUR SOFT FURNISHINGS

Machine wash or dry-clean curtains, depending on instructions. Ditto loose fabrics. You could swap heavy, dark loose covers (and curtains if you are very lucky) from your winter to your spring collection. Now turn to your sofa. Give cushions a good old bashing outside to remove dust, and you may need to take a warm cloth to the under-the-cushion area. Collect and sort lost items. Buy a nice scented candle with all that money you find.

WIPE AND WASH

Wipe all walls and ceilings and remove grease or stains. Dust and wipe clean all doors and handles. Handles harbour all kinds of germs and need a regular wipe.

BUST THE DUST

Suck up all the dust on the floor with a vacuum cleaner, making sure you go behind furniture and into corners.

Remove all books and ornaments from shelves and use a feather duster to dust both. If they are very dirty, they may need a wash or wipe. Prune or mend anything that is broken or beyond repair and 'left on the shelf', and de-clutter. Get to know the crevice tool on your vacuum. Dust your room from top to bottom, in that order.

SEE IT THROUGH

Give all windows and mirrors a clean, inside and out, with vinegar and hot water. Wipe all blinds with a hot cloth. Wipe all sills, cleaning under any items on there and not round. Check that any plants are still alive and put them out of their misery if not.

WIPE 'N' WAX

Wipe wooden surfaces with a soft cloth and then polish or wax till you can see your smug smile reflected in it!

PULL THE RUG OUT

Sweep non-carpeted floors from edge to edge, moving furniture as required. Do not cut corners by sweeping around furniture. Deep clean carpets and rugs with a shampoo machine.

STAMP ON THE DAMP, LICK THE LIMESCALE

Mould, mildew and limescale sound like a firm of accountants employed by Mr Scrooge. And if they've set up shop in your home, you'll want to get rid of them pronto as they are unsightly, a bit depressing and not good for your health.

You will need

Respiratory mask
Bleach
White vinegar
Lemon
Spray bottle
Cloth
Plastic scourer
Anti-mould spray

MESSRS MOULD AND MILDEW

Caused by spores in the air that grow in damp areas where there's little air circulation, mould and mildew can be harmful to health, particularly to asthma sufferers, so wear a respiratory mask when you treat them.

- Wipe or rub with a solution of one part bleach in two parts water, but proprietary cleaners are also available.
- Once clean and dry, treat the area with an anti-mould spray to try and prevent the spores settling again.
- Anti-mould paints are also available. If wallpaper is attacked by mould, it may be more effective to remove the section affected. Apply an anti-mould treatment to the wall before re-papering.
- If mould gets into carpet (or upholstery), it is difficult to remove and leaves an unpleasant smell. The carpet (and probably underlay) should really be replaced, or at least the section affected. Otherwise, spray the carpet with white vinegar, rub and dry it off, but even professional carpet cleaning will not remove mould completely.

DAMP VS CONDENSATION

Rising damp Found at the base of walls and skirting boards. Possibly due to poor drainage or a problem with a damp-proof course, such as the ground outside being above the damp-proof course. You need expert advice.

Damp caused by leaks May come from cracks in walls or damaged pipes. Leaks can originate further away from where the damp patch is visible, and not just from directly above – look diagonally or even horizontally. If you can't find the culprit, seek advice.

Damp caused by condensation Mainly due to warm moist air meeting a colder surface where it condenses – steamy kitchens and bathrooms provide optimal conditions – just opening windows should help. Move cupboards away from walls to allow air to circulate; dry clothes outside if possible; keep extractor fans on for several minutes after cooking; or use a dehumidifier. If the problem persists, seek advice.

MS LIMESCALE

In hard water areas, this is the white/greenish deposit that accumulates around taps and on shower basins and baths. You can buy proprietary cleaners but vinegar and lemon also do the trick – they need to be in contact with the offending area for several hours or overnight. Soak a cloth in vinegar and wrap it around the area that needs treating. Use the pulp as well as the juice of a lemon – jam a half lemon onto the end of a tap and leave overnight. Wash off and scrub any stubborn bits with a plastic scourer.

CHAPTER THREE
STYLE ON A SHOESTRING

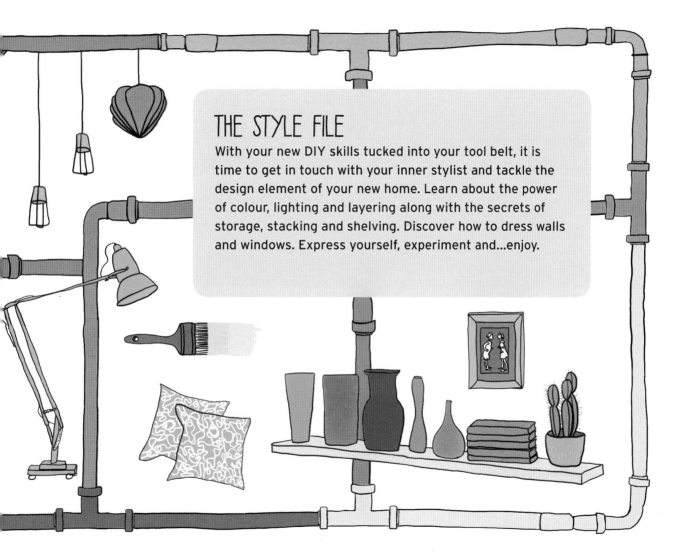

THE STYLE FILE

With your new DIY skills tucked into your tool belt, it is time to get in touch with your inner stylist and tackle the design element of your new home. Learn about the power of colour, lighting and layering along with the secrets of storage, stacking and shelving. Discover how to dress walls and windows. Express yourself, experiment and...enjoy.

IN THE MOOD

Mood boards are a great way to plan your colour scheme. Inspirational and practical, they save time and money in the long run – Sensational Scarlet may sound like a fun idea on paper, but could cause red faces and bank balances in real life.

CREATE YOUR OWN MOOD BOARD

Collect articles from magazines and catalogues, fabric and paint swatches (including top-of-the-range), cuttings from carpets, textiles and wallpaper. Don't go round cutting chunks out of other people's curtains, but take photographs of houses you admire, places you visit that inspire, room sets in stores or at exhibitions that you love. Even seed packets, food and cosmetic packaging or labels with appealing designs can kick-start your colour creativity. Be a mood board magpie at first and create a collage or an ideas box of different swatches and pieces; then streamline into a mood board with a dominant theme. Go one step further if you like, and sketch a floor plan and transfer elements onto it so you can really visualize it.

Check out the various online digital mood boards and create a virtual board. Take advantage of the huge range of ideas at your fingertips. Upload and share your work in progress. Get feedback from your partner and friends (and of course from any fellow housemates). Ask any contacts you may have in the profession to be soundboards for your pinboard.

TRY BEFORE YOU BUY; REPAINT EQUALS REPENT

Invest in small pots of paint or borrow leftover paint from friends in colours that catch your eye, and paint or attach small swatches on discreet areas of the wall. You could even create and put up a mini mood board.

FIND YOUR OWN STYLE

Pinpointing your own 'interiors voice' can be a bit daunting. If you are struggling with your personal style, scribble down a few keywords that spring to mind in terms of your general leanings and preferences. Canvass opinion from friends. Don't worry, these first ideas are not set in designer stone, but will get the style ball rolling.

Boho chic Do I like to have lots of accessories in a colourful, messy-tidy, rule-breaker style?

Eclectic traveller Do I want to display my collections from trips to various countries with different styles, fabrics and touches of the exotic?

Vintage Do I like lots of found objects and reclaimed stuff in a sort of shabby-chic, salvage, retro-glam style?

Hygge Do I want the look to be all Danish-style cosy warmth, with painted wooden floors, natural materials, lovely blankets and plenty of candles?

Country cottage Do I like soft colours, floral fabrics and pretty throws on the sofa, in an 'urban patchwork' style?

Scandi-minimalist Do I like the idea of a tidy environment with calm colours, clean lines and just a few key pieces?

COLOUR IT IN

Deciding on a colour scheme for your home may be scary but you have nothing to fear from the palette. There is no right or wrong when choosing a hero hue (a main room colour – not your life partner), but understanding a few basic principles should give you the confidence to reveal your own true colours.

HOW COLOURS RELATE

Take a spin in the colour wheel (and go on a trip back to school): equidistant from one another are the three primary colours – red, yellow and blue – which form the basis for all others. The primaries cannot be made from other colours, but when mixed together they can create any other colour. Then come the three secondary hues, orange, purple and green, the result of mixing two primary colours (such as blue with red to form purple). They sit on the wheel between those colours that make them. The more subtle tertiary colours nestle between the primary and secondary ones used to create them and have double-barrelled names, such as red-orange or blue-green. You could go on mixing colours but things might get muddy.

Colour harmonies Created by using three colours situated at equal distances from each other on the wheel (e.g., red, blue and yellow – think Vermeer's *Girl with a Pearl Earring*). Adjacent or analogous colour harmony is achieved with three colours that sit side-by-side on the wheel (yellow-green, yellow and yellow-orange for example – think Van Gogh's *Sunflowers*).

Complementary colours Any two colours directly opposite each other on the wheel (red and green, yellow and purple, red-purple and yellow-green – you will have seen them in adverts). These create drama and contrast and are good for intense flashes of colour. Monochromatic colours are all the tints, shades and tones of a single hue (think Picasso's blue period or *Guernica*). They can look very sophisticated but you will probably want to introduce contrasting texture, pattern or shades of colour to bring visual interest to a room.

Primaries

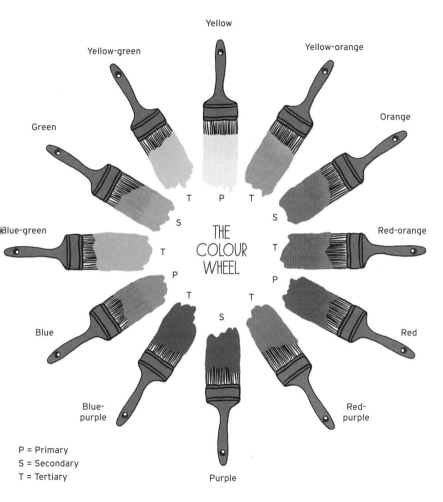

Yellow

Yellow-green   Yellow-orange

Green   Orange

                        T   P   T
                            S
Blue-green   THE   S   Red-orange
                    COLOUR
                    WHEEL   T
               T   P
               P   T   T
                            S
Blue   Red

Blue-   Red-
purple   purple

P = Primary
S = Secondary
T = Tertiary

Purple

WARMER OR COLDER?

Colours are also classified as either warm or cool: red, yellow and orange, browns, tans and beige/cream are on the warm team (think sunny day out with friends). They tend to appeal to our emotions and work well in a cosy, intimate living room or kitchen where we do most of our socializing. Blue, green, purple/lilac and grey play it cool (a quiet, cloudy day in); they appeal more to the intellect, helping us to relax and achieve calm and focus, while also increasing the sense of space; they can be a good choice in bedrooms and offices.

FEELING NEUTRAL

Neutrals can get a bad rap for being rather dull, but they work well in small rooms, bringing both a sense of calm and the illusion of space. Warm neutrals include brown, cream and taupe, whereas grey, blue and white are cool. Within a neutral décor you can play with texture in fabrics and shape in furniture, and introduce varying shades of your chosen neutral.

IN THE COLOUR SCHEME OF THINGS

Now that you have brushed up on the colour wheel (various apps can jog your memory if you need to refer to it on the hoof), check out magazines, websites, artworks, friends' homes and even nature itself for inspiration. Make the palette principles work for you. Juggle with colour; don't be jinxed by it.

Making the right choice

When choosing colours, think about the function of each room, how long you will spend in it and what ambience you want. And how big it is. Is it a small, dark room that you want to make feel brighter and bigger? How about a cosy and intimate living room, a cool, calm bedroom and a busy, bright kitchen? Or a neutral décor that flows through two or more rooms, with a few splashes of vibrant colour?

Try before you buy

There are hundreds of shades of each colour (some with fairly fanciful names) so get hold of swatches and small pots of paint and try them out, in daylight, under artificial light and at different times of the day. Baby Elephant Grey or Dying Swan White may not have the same appeal on a misty Monday morning as on a sunlit Saturday afternoon.

In the scheme of things

Colour schemes generally involve two or three colours. As a starting point, choose your first colour from the wheel and look at the one opposite: this could be your second colour. You can introduce a third colour but more and you are heading on the way to a headache or back to your teenage bedroom. Be wary of garish. The designer rule decrees that 60 per cent of the room should be in the dominant colour, 30 per cent in the secondary one and 10 per cent in an accent hue (in the form of furnishings or accessories). It is about balance and moderation and what makes you feel good.

If you are not feeling bold about being bold, consider shades of a neutral colour for a softer and calmer feel. This is your home, a sanctuary not a show-off showroom. It is up to you if you go maxi, multi, mono or mini in terms of colour. And it is not set in any shade of stone. You can change it when your mood and budget allow.

The right shade of pale

Paler colours appear to recede, thereby making rooms look bigger. In a small room you could paint your floorboards and walls in cool and pale colours to deliver space and calm. Bolder colours tend to come forward and while they may make spaces appear smaller they can also make a room very cosy. A bold accent colour on one wall works well if you are looking for quick bit of oomph rather than a total makeover.

GLOSSARY

Tint = colour + white

Shade = colour + black

Tone = colour + neutral

Accent colour = used in small quantities to add a pop of colour to the décor

YOUR FOUR WALLS

Walls offer your inner artist the perfect canvas. Not for graffiti perhaps, although using stylish wall lettering is a trendy option. Walls make bold statements or subtle backgrounds. Clad in tiles, paint, panels or paper, like guests at a party, they can start conversations or hang back discreetly.

WHAT WORKS WHERE

Tongue-and-groove MDF wood panelling or reclaimed wood applied with your new skills can introduce style/shabby chic to a living or dining space. Tiles impress in kitchens and bathrooms (See Big It Up, page 78), but don't rule out wallpaper here. A coating of decorator's varnish to protect it from grease, a sheet of Plexiglas as a splashback or washable vinyl wallpaper can fix things in these functional rooms. If you go for wallpaper, always try swatches before investing to check it matches your paint/furniture and how it looks in different lights. Wall designs affect the visual space in a room.

ON A ROLL OR A BRUSH

Stripes can make smaller rooms look bigger: horizontal ones lengthen walls and vertical ones lift a low ceiling. A feature wall with a dramatic print makes a great focal point in a room (floral or geometric perhaps). A smallish 3D-effect design can bring style to a small space but huge flowers or dramatic shapes on all four walls will not just catch eyes but bring tears to them. A diagonal on a single wall can also enlarge a room. Make an alcove go wow with a bold colour or pattern. Paint the ceiling the same colour as the walls or a couple of shades lighter to increase the sense of space. A careful combination of wall, lighting and your artwork will get everyone talking.

AN EYE FOR DIY

Design your own wallpaper by uploading a photo to one of the many digital printing sites (and then sell your masterpiece online). How about enjoying your favourite view in the bathroom or bedroom as a trompe l'oeil? Alternatively, simply stick your own cutouts on a wall or apply vinyl wall decals to a dull corner. Chalkboard paint can help to unleash your inner Banksy or Pollock.

EFFECTIVE EFFECTS

Tile, wood or brick-effect wallpaper brings style without the slog (although you could try your hand at painting these faux effects). If you are lucky enough have exposed bricks, celebrate them au naturel in NY loft apartment style or paint in distressed white or   a soft, subtle grey.

For renters, temporary wallpaper that can be easily removed or plain removable wallpaper onto which you can add your own collage or design deliver practical solutions.

LIGHT IT UP

Lighting is an undervalued multitasker. It creates atmosphere, enhances mood and increases the sense of space; it pinpoints, highlights and flatters (and stops you walking into the furniture). There is no need to spend a fortune on expensive fixtures; just get switched on to the basic types and functions of lighting.

GUIDING LIGHTS

Different kinds of lighting are available and it is good to mix and match them in each room. Start with ambient lighting and then think about how to introduce others. Layering (different kinds of lights in different positions) is the way to go but leave the wiring stuff to the professionals.

Ambient or general Natural light or light from fixtures that illuminates your room and establishes the basic light level and mood.

Task Lighting for specific jobs such as reading, cooking and close-up work.

Accent or feature Focused lighting that highlights an interesting item, detail or feature.

Security or utility Lighting inside wardrobes and cupboards or outside the home (see Keeping An Eye On Things, page 100).

COOL AND POOL

Exposed filament bulbs without a shade but with decorative flexes deliver retro-industrial chic and a warm light. Fairy and festoon lights draped round a mantelpiece, wall or shelf, or even inside a Kilner jar, sprinkle romantic stardust into a room. Strategic low lighting (from a lamp) in a corner against a dark wall makes an interesting focal point. And there is always the disco mirror ball for party nights...

ROOM BY ROOM

When choosing lighting for a particular room, consider size, function (work/sleep/relaxation/entertainment), frequency or length of use (need for energy-efficiency lighting) and desired mood. Have you got a lovely painting you would like to show off?

Dining room/area Pendant lighting that does not obstruct the view of guests works well (a chandelier would certainly make a statement), with dimmer switches for atmosphere and candles to flatter, relax and romance.

Kitchens Layer different lights in this very functional space and try to establish a light for each working zone (recessed or protected from grease where necessary). Under-cupboard lighting is effective for food prep areas and you might even want to splash out on a backlit, tiled splashback in a dark sink area (works in the bathroom too); light-reflecting paint in dark kitchens also helps.

Living area Combine ambient lighting for relaxation with accent lighting on a particular area or feature (a painting, for example), plus task lighting for reading. Strip lights can transform shelving into a feature and uplighters will focus on architectural features while enhancing ambience.

Bedroom Go for accent lighting rather than ambient. Bedside angled lamps are useful, but if you need to save space mount task lighting on walls instead.

Office Overhead and task lighting are practical solutions in a hard-working area. Angled desk and oversized floor lamps deliver a targeted pool of light while looking stylish.

JAZZ IT UP

Gorgeous gauze or voluptuous velvet? Roman, Venetian or naked? It all sounds a little saucy but these are some of your window-dressing options, budget permitting. If you have a view to die for and no nosy neighbours, try the undressed route. It's always reversible.

WHICH TREATMENT?

Room by room, answer the following questions.

- Do I want to hide the view or enjoy it?
- How much privacy do I need?
- Do I need to make the most of the light source?
- Does the room need to be dark (for sleeping)?
- Do I need to draughtproof this area?

SEEING AND BEING SEEN

A window with no treatment can impress from both sides of the pane, and of course allows the maximum amount of light to pour in. If you go 'window commando', make sure you keep the glass and its frame clean and well maintained. Muslin, voile or sheer fabric provides protection from glare-'n'-stare without stealing too much light. Heavy curtains deliver privacy and a cosy feel plus insulation, but they do inhibit light, demand cleaning from time to time and can cost more, but you should be able to pick up some pre-loved ones fairly easily.

BLIND AMBITION

There are several types of blind, most of which are available in a range of colours, some quite funky (e.g. metallic and neon). And if you have yet to get some drill skills under your belt (see page 12), check out the click-in blinds that are drill-free and child-safe. Instant paper blinds are available for quick solutions to your window wardrobe problems.

A GLOSSARY OF BLINDS

Roller Simple, relatively cheap, practical and easy to clean, these do what they say on the tin but are not always the poor relations. They work well in kitchens and bathrooms and can be almost invisible when rolled up, thereby leaving views intact. They can also offer a blank, sheer canvas on which to add your own stylistic touches. In a bay window, a simple blind in a neutral colour allows the window to make its own architectural statement. Bamboo roller blinds deliver a natural, organic look and can be eco-friendly. Check out blind fabrics with built-in anti-microbial, anti-fungal properties too. Blackout blinds are great for light sleepers and nurseries, and can be much more stylish than you might think.

Roman These pleated fabric blinds can add a decorative touch to windows and are even relatively easy to make, allowing you to match décor and fabric. Ready-made versions come in a range of great colours and fabrics.

Venetian So-called because they were created in Italy, these blinds have horizontal slats that can be adjusted to regulate light and privacy. Available in a host of designs and colours and mostly in aluminium, PVC and vinyl, they are impressive but relatively inexpensive. Blackout Venetian blinds are also available for extra darkness.

Vertical These blinds have vertical slats (the name is a giveaway) and again come in different colours, fabrics and widths.

Window film This is an easy and instant alternative and comes in stylish designs (not just frost effect), and with solar control properties. Works well in kitchens, bathrooms and on internal doors/windows. And what about quirky window decals in the smallest room?

IS IT CURTAINS FOR CURTAINS?

Curtain-ly not. They can offer seclusion, snugness and sophistication in a whole heap of fabrics: lightweight or heavy, semi-transparent (gauze, muslin, voile or lace) or with more light control (velvet or heavy cotton). They can be sheer, shimmering or substantial, discreet or dramatic, varying in length like gowns, from just below the sill to romantic floor-length or trailing cascade. Pleated or straight, on tracks or poles, curtains bring flourishes or pools of colour, flashes or floods of pattern into a room. They can match your furnishings and décor or offer a strong contrast, delivering drama and texture to a minimalist room, for example. And they can be used in combination with blinds.

Here are a few curtain calls for smaller rooms:

- Mount the curtain rod as close to the ceiling as you can to make the window space appear bigger. Extend the curtain rod beyond the width of the window, too, to trick the eye.
- Curtains in a similar colour to the walls make the window area seem bigger. They don't have to match exactly.
- Short curtains can reduce the height of a room visually.
- Curtains make useful room dividers (see Home Office Job, page 90) and can be used to hide collections of unsightly equipment, household items or ugly white goods.

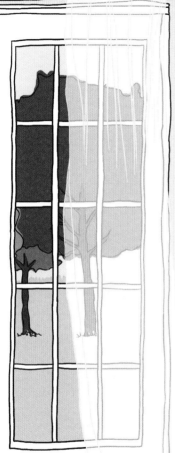

OPEN OR SHUTTER CASE?

Unless you inherit lovely wooden shutters with your home, these are quite an investment, but first hunt around in salvage shops. They are available in all kinds of materials (wood, vinyl, glass, MDF, Perspex, fabric, bamboo), provide privacy, soundproofing and insulation and are easy to keep clean.

They can be louvred with slats that are fixed or operable (i.e. adjustable), and come as full height, tier-on-tier (stable door style), café-type (covering the lower portion of the window), plantation (wooden with wider slats) or solid. Consider what you want from your shutters in terms of delivering privacy, style and light before investing in new ones.

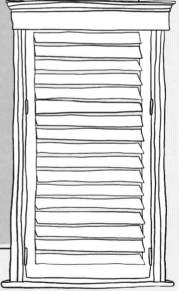

BIG IT UP

Mirrors big up rooms. They bounce reflected light around (both natural light and light from lamps) and increase space visually, drawing the eye. Mirrors light up dark corners, add depth to a room and widen the view. Interior designers love them.

THE STRAIGHT AND NARROW

Mirrors work well in narrow spaces. Position a floor mirror in your hall as tall as the wall and hey presto, not all smoke and mirrors, the room seems bigger. Or hang a long mirror horizontally in a dark narrow space. It is worth investing a little time and money in searching out an old or pre-loved mirror or a salvaged antique to upcycle.

REFLECTED GLORY

Make a statement wall by leaning a full-length mirror against it and placing several smaller ones above. Or hang a collection of mirrors in different shapes and sizes and paint the frames in a single, standout hero hue as a mini mirror gallery, or even the same colour as the wall. Hang rectangular mirrors horizontally and vertically with regular spacing for a stylish effect.

REFLECTION OF PERFECTION

Mirrors reflect what they see so always position yours with that in mind. Reflecting a large pile of mess equals two piles of mess. Instead position one opposite a great view, a lovely painting or photograph. Placing a mirror between two windows creates the illusion of a third. Frame a mirror to look like a window in a dark space or try a fish-eye convex mirror that reflects the whole room back at you. Beware too many mirrors in a small room as it can feel a bit like a funfair when several friends come round.

with a simple sheet of glass supported on pale bricks, books or wood. Choose light furniture rather than heavy, pale rather than dark wood, and aim to keep the same flooring through different rooms, such as stripped back, natural or painted floorboards, to increase visual flow.

Kitchen Mirror tiles work well as splashbacks in the kitchen. Clear glass tiles (with no visible grouting) are very effective; self-adhesive mirror sticker tiles are an easier option. Metallic taps, door handles and other reflective surfaces and accessories also bounce natural light around.

Bathroom Mirror tiles increase light and space in a bathroom but position with care to reflect a pretty plant rather than less attractive items! Silver, mirrored or 3D tiles big up the smallest room but can dent a small budget. Install a glass shower door or transparent curtain along with nice shiny taps and cupboard handles. Budding bathroom Botticellis could try their hand at painting a trompe l'oeil window in a windowless bathroom. Let there be light!

MIRRORS ROOM BY ROOM

Living room Install a mirror in an empty fireplace with some candles for a flickering Scandinavian-style, cosy 'hygge' feel. A mirror on the wall alongside your kitchen or dining table creates a romantic, moody-food dining atmosphere. Line the wall behind shelves with mirrors or position mirrors among your bookshelves. Glass tabletops or acrylic stools and tables reflect the light and vanish visually. Make your own table

FILL IT IN

When arranging your ABC of stuff –
accessories, books and collections
of ornaments, photos and paintings,
and so on – express your personality.
This is a home, not a museum or a gallery.
You are displaying, not exhibiting, your
possessions. Don't feel pressurized to
adopt a certain style or trend. It's all about
balance, a few design principles and being
able to count.

BREAKING THE RULES

There are guidelines on how to
arrange your personal possessions, but
no set rules. The first rule is that you don't
need to follow one: this is your home, and
your accessories are records of your holidays,
achievements, interests and family, both past
and present. You are the curator of the
pieces you put on display and you can
update the collection as your tastes,
trends and travels develop.

THE POWER OF THREE

The basic design rule is that things
arranged in odd numbers (say, three)
work better than in even ones (say,
two or four). The rule of thirds used in
photographic composition is a useful
rule of designer thumb. Grouping odd
numbers together creates visual interest
and cohesion, making what is essentially
a staged arrangement ironically look
more natural, as the eye travels around
the grouping of things. Vary the height,
size, shape and texture of items (such
as a collection of ornaments) but try
to link them in some way, to establish
a common theme, a colour or style for
example. Same but different and in odd
numbers – give it a try. And if you don't
like it, change it. The style enforcers
won't come knocking on your quirky door.

ECLECTIC VS MINIMALIST

Eclectic tendencies are interesting and creative, but beware the small leap from judicious juggle to messy jumble. And (with your maths head back on) consider scale. If space is limited, think in threes rather than fives or sevens. If you are more of a minimalist and less keen on accessories, try placing three of your prized ceramics on a console table. Deduct one and see how it looks. Either way, minis and maxis should make like a pro, take a photo and decide how to go. It will all start to add up.

LAYERS, NOT LINES

In design terms there is no need to put all your ducks in a very symmetrical row. In fact, it is a good idea not to if you want to establish some visual interest. Layering instead of lining up delivers depth. Try making a small display or vignette on a table in a dull corner and layer three items, tall at the back, smaller to the side, another in front, placing them in different positions until you like the result. It works on the wall as well. Two paintings side by side can look a bit lost but when joined by more, you have a gallery (see Hang It All, page 82).

HANG IT ALL

From prints, posters and photos to certificates, maps and ancestral portraits, pictures personalize and decorate a room. Here are some tips for positioning and hanging them.

WHERE?

Try a picture in different positions around the room. If you have a helpful assistant, get them to hold it up so you can stand back and view it from a metre or so away. When you've decided, mark the position of the two top corners of the picture on the wall lightly in pencil.

If you're home alone, cut out a piece of paper the size of the picture and, providing it won't damage or mark the surface, stick it on the wall in its potential position. Try small blobs of reusable putty adhesive, Command strips, painter's tape (some painter's tapes can be used on delicate surfaces such as wallpaper), or just use ordinary dressmaker's pins, which leave only tiny holes.

GROUPS

If you're hanging a group of pictures, treat them as a single unit and centre them within the space available. Pictures of the same size look neat hung in an orderly row. Cut out a piece of paper the size of each picture and lay them on the floor to try out different combinations, the largest in the centre. Now look at them from a high vantage point, even if it's only standing on a chair.

POSITION POINTERS

Where you hang a picture is a matter of taste, but if you'd like some general guidance, try these tips.

- Position the picture so its centre is at or a little below eye level. In the event of an unseemly scuffle between taller and shorter members of the household as to exactly where this is, opt to position the centre of the picture around 150cm/approx. 60in from the floor.
- Avoid direct sunlight for delicate images (particularly if you've high hopes of your bargain from the junk shop turning out to be a lost Picasso) and areas of high humidity (which may cause the picture to buckle).
- If hanging over a table or a sofa, leave a gap of at least 10–20cm/ 4–8in between furniture and the bottom of the picture.

WHAT'S MY WALL?

Unless you are hanging one of the Elgin marbles, or an old master in a big, blowsy frame, weight may not be an issue, but what your wall is made of will affect the fixing you use (see pages 16–17).

SHELF LIFE

Shelves can perform their function in cupboards or behind a curtain if necessary, or do their 'store and show' in style, displaying your books, photos, prized pieces and possessions. They can be made from a whole shelfload of materials: solid wood, plywood, plastic, glass, metal, wire, MDF, driftwood, salvaged pallets or scaffolding boards, fence slats or crates. You can suspend them with wires from the wall or ceiling, use ropes or even plumbing pipes as supports, or just plump for wooden or metallic brackets. Go rustic, warehouse industrial, traditional or quirky. Paint the shelves in a bright colour to stand out from the wall (neon shelves can look very funky) or the same hue for a more subtle effect. Floating shelves have concealed brackets but are best for light loads, such as a few books or mementos. Painted to match the wall, they look even more invisible, taking up less visual space in a small room.

PUT IT UP

Shelves are functional and flexible; they can be fashionable, too. They can be free-standing with adjustable brackets (great for renters), or fixed. A shelving unit can divide a room and be a feature in itself. Finished by your own fair hands (see Pack It In, page 56) or fashioned by them, shelves are your friend.

HANGING ON IN THERE

Make sure your selected shelf system can support the planned weight and won't pull away from the wall, or worse still, collapse and bring some of the wall down with it. Choose suitable brackets (you may need more than two for a long shelf) and fixings. If the wall is plasterboard rather than solid, use a multipurpose detector to find the studs; mark their positions so you can fix the brackets to those. Place a bracket against the wall at the correct height and make a mark on the wall through the hole for the fixing in the bracket. Drill the wall and insert a fixing to hold the bracket in place. Check it is level with a spirit level. Balance one end of the shelf on this bracket, place a spirit level on top and mark the position for the bracket at the opposite end of the shelf. Remove the shelf and fix the second bracket. The shelf can simply rest on top of the bracket, but can also be fixed to the bracket for additional security.

You will need
(See pages 12–17 for fixings and drilling)

Shelf (of suitable material, cut to size)
Suitable brackets (to support the shelf)
Suitable fixings (for the weight of the shelf)
Spirit level
Drill
Pencil or marker

Check the shelf is level before inserting any additional fixings in the brackets.

The longest part of the bracket normally goes against the wall.

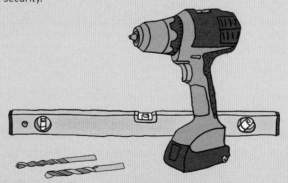

STASH IT

Your new home will need to house you and everything you own (that is not in an attic belonging to accommodating friends or family). When space is at a premium, being storage-savvy is vital. If you moved in without decluttering, now is the time to prune your possessions, weed out clothes you haven't worn or things you haven't used in the last year (or six months).

ROOM BY ROOM

Look at each room and its storage potential. Think high and low, vertical and horizontal: walls and floors, under, inside and even behind furniture, above and beneath cupboards. Ceilings are perfect for attaching a hoist for your bike or hanging a wardrobe rail. Get your storage-smart thinking cap on (removing it from the helpful hook in the hallway first).

Hallway Hook it, bench it

Hallways are clutter magnets but can house useful storage. Coat hooks come in a huge range of stylish designs and materials. Choose or paint yours to match the walls or in fun colours to brighten a dark area. Track down an old bench, add wicker or plastic baskets below and shelves above, and voilà: storage for boots, sports and outdoor gear, umbrellas, shopping bags, bike helmets and your folding bike.

UNSIGHTLY STORAGE

Out of sight can be out of mind. A pretty screen or a simple curtain can cover storage that is not picture-perfect.

Bedroom Box it, sleep on it

Storing things under the bed is a good idea, but do so methodically, after folding and even vacuum-wrapping chosen items (not just any old stuff without a home). Make use of any built-in drawers, or source plastic, wicker, wooden or salvaged containers (after measuring). Make a box out of wood with your new DIY skills. Attach wheels and handles for ease of removal and replacement. Fasten a cover over the top for extra protection from dust. If you are investing in a new bed, consider an ottoman divan with all its wonderful under-mattress storage potential. Could you aim high with a mid- or high-sleeper bed, leaving oodles of lovely space for storage below? Putting a lovely old trunk at the end of your bed could provide extra storage and surface space.

Make space work hard in the bedroom: a bedside table complete with shelves and/or drawers for books, tablets and phones, a light mounted on the wall that frees up surface space, hooks inside your wardrobe for scarves, ties or hairdryers. An over-the-door shoe rack prevents the bottom of the wardrobe or the floor looking down at heel. In the absence of a wardrobe, hang clothes on a rail suspended from the ceiling or fit a simple corner rail. Think vertically, horizontally, laterally (and tidily). A place for everything and everything in its place.

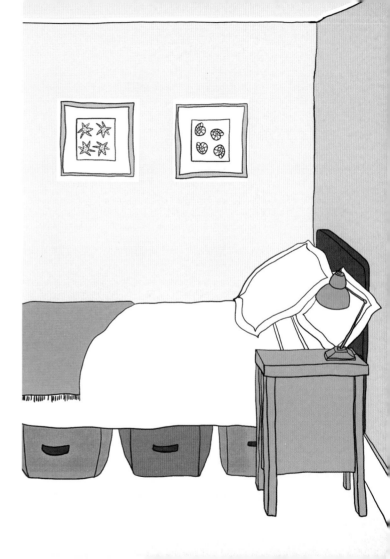

ROOM BY ROOM (CONTINUED)

Kitchens and living rooms have to cope with a lot of clutter, especially if they are being used as multifunctional spaces, so be creative and always allow for more storage than you think you will need.

Living room Store it, shelve it

You may spend most of your time in this room, so be as storage-savvy as possible, while respecting it as a space for relaxation and entertaining. When choosing furniture (new, upcycled or reclaimed), go for items that multitask. Trunks make good surfaces for books and support bottoms. A pre-loved ottoman with a hinged lid stores throws, cushions, blankets and guests (on top!). Stacked crates house magazines and give a TV a home. Choose a coffee table with drawers or stylish storage room below. Could you fit shelving/baskets/plastic boxes behind the sofa (or is your home office there, see page 90)?

Shelve your books not your ideas. Ceiling-to-floor shelves work well both as a focal point and a home for those with many tomes. Free-standing open shelving can divide rooms cleverly at the same time (see Home Office Job, pages 90). Turn a bookshelf on its side and insert baskets if you want to lower your storage horizons. Create some shelves in an old upended wooden drawer. Corner shelves make use of what can be 'dead' space, and shelving can even be attached to windowsills with hinges.

Kitchen Take the high load or the low load

This is the most hardworking room and surface space is in high demand. Aim low. Remove doors from a dresser, cupboards or chest of drawers to store pots and pans in some open storage.

Clear the lost, unused space under fitted cupboards to store trays and tins. How about a foldout table for food prep and consumption, and collapsible chairs hooked on the walls, Shaker-style? When buying/bidding for a kitchen/dining table, look for one with built-in 'secret storage' for cutlery, placemats, etc. or at least one with drawers. Make a table out of reclaimed wood mounted securely on cabinets or shelves.

Aim high. Add a magnetic strip to a wall to store knives without taking up surface space. Store items you don't use much on the highest shelves (install as many shelves as you have room for), ordering them by regularity of use: daily to once in a blue moon. Fix handles to boxes so that you can move them more easily.

ROCK THE RACK

The pegboard has come out of the garage to deliver a splash of colour and a whole heap of organization. Made of acrylic, metal, hardboard or wood, and adorned with a host of hooks and holders, it is at home on cupboard doors for vertical storage of equipment (consider weight issues), accessories and tools. Hang pans in the kitchen, clothes and jewellery in the bedroom and cosmetics in the bathroom. Available as pegboard sheets (cut to size), mount them just about anywhere (but not above the oven for fire risk reasons) using your new drill skills (see pages 14–15). Paint in the colour of your choice with a thin layer of an easy-to-wipe paint but avoid filling in the holes (a roller is probably easiest). Chalkboard paint can look quirky in the kitchen.

HOME OFFICE JOB

You will need

Lighting/light source
Power source
Comfortable chair
Workable surface
Storage

MAKE SPACE WORK FOR YOU

The answers to these questions will help you create your perfect office.

- 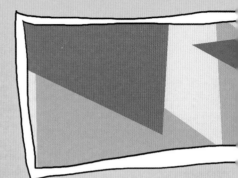 How many hours a day will I work here?
- Is it comfortable enough for full- or part-time work?
- Will I have to share it?
- Will I disturb housemates?
- Am I a tidy worker?
- Can I work in a fold-away/ put-away office?
- How paperless is my job and can I live without a printer?

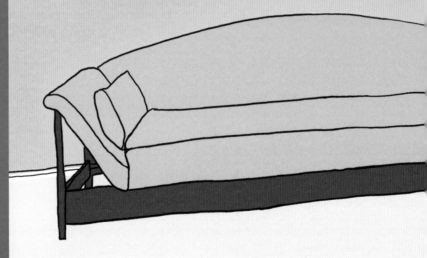

DIVIDE AND CONQUER

In a living room or bedroom you could zone off your work area with a screen, curtain, bookshelf or filing cabinet on wheels (at desk height, preferably, or it could invade the space rather than divide it). A freestanding set of shelves can perform three roles by storing books, files and equipment – tidily – while creating an important physical barrier and hiding potential mess.

Room dividers can be as simple, stunning or solid as your finances and preferences permit. Hanging screens come in lovely designs, while curtains can be as easy as sheer fabric on a strip of wire to more luxurious or even pre-loved drapes. A pretty canvas, bamboo or Shoji screen does the job nicely without blocking out too much light and can be folded away if necessary. Paint a reclaimed wooden screen to match the rest of the room if you want to blend in, or go bold to make more of a visual statement piece or upcycle an old screen with pretty fabric (in different colours on either side for extra design versatility).

HARD-WORKING AREAS

Dual spaces are very much the norm now and if you have limited space you may have to install your workstation/office in a room with an existing function. Make maximum and clever use of the space available and be prepared to be as organized as possible, particularly in a house share. Be as tidy as you can or mess will start to build up.

LOCATION, VOCATION

Think creatively about establishing an office space in the smallest or most unlikely of places. You might have a built-in wardrobe or closet wide and deep enough to take a desk. Could you convert a wardrobe or armoire with your new DIY skills, making shelving and a drop-leaf desk? Would a fold-out desk in your bedroom, some under-the-bed storage and a comfortable chair suffice? You might be able to use a space at the end of the bed for a simple desk. Could you fit an L-shaped desk into a corner of the kitchen or make your own desk to fit into an irregular, awkward shape? Use corkboards or pegboards on the door or the inside of cupboards for storage. Check/measure/sketch on paper the hallway or entrance and see if it could house a desk. Remember that you will need proper lighting in a windowless area. Be canny in any cranny and look for dead space, such as an area under a flight of stairs. Pull the sofa away from the wall in the living room and put a table and chair in the space with some floating shelves for files and books. Build or buy some wall shelves, fixing one that extends at the right height to form a desk. Appropriate the dining table temporarily/semi-permanently. Invest in a small, mobile, Z-shaped or folding workstation that can be wheeled in and out of a room as required; some have a built-in shelf or storage.

TIPS FOR A HAPPY HOME OFFICE LIFE

- Invest in a supportive chair at the correct height: it can double up as a living room chair with a throw and cushions.

- Ensure your computer is at the right height and with enough room on the supporting surface for your keyboard, key accessories and elbows.

- Be as organized and tidy as possible with discreet storage boxes and attractive files.

- Use cable ties for leads and chargers to avoid Spaghetti Junction on the floor.

- Use natural light where possible and invest in some angle/wall lights.

- Keep the floor clear and don't use it as an in- or out-tray.

- Consider working in calm colours rather than looking at very bright ones for several hours a day.

THE MOBILE OFFICE

A discreet wall-mounted desk or a pull-out, flip-down, fold-away one, a laptop that sleeps in its case, a couple of floating shelves you can appropriate and some task lighting: now you see your secret study, now you don't.

SWAP IT, PAINT IT, STICK IT

You will be surprised at just how easy it is to update features and furniture with a few fabulous flashes of inspiration. Introduce a new look into a room with inexpensive accessories or pre-loved fabrics. Risk a fun facelift without getting into the red.

A LICK OR SPRAY OF PAINT

Just painting a single wall a statement hue or brightening a dark alcove with a bold colour can bring a smile to a room without breaking the bank. Paint an internal door an experimental colour or update the front door; paint a fun design on your hallway floorboards (checking any necessary permissions first: paint is hard to remove from floorboards). It will feel like a new home next time you enter. Revamp the kitchen with newly painted cupboards. All in a Saturday's work.

GET A HANDLE ON COLOUR

On a smaller scale, simply add some fun handles or knobs to a chest of drawers or kitchen cabinet. Spray paint them in a range of attention-grabbing colours (including metallic for extra bling) after a proper degrease, degrime and prime. An antique brass finish could work well (and brings new life to tired taps). Keep an eye out for unusual designs of knobs, handles and taps at flea markets and antique shops. Paint each drawer on a chest of drawers a different standout shade or add a selection of handles to a monochrome one. Mix and match in your mini makeover and release your inner artist/rebel/bohemian.

UPDATE NOT EXTERMINATE

Rather than replacing them, breathe fresh life into tired laminate countertops with paint. Try a granite-effect or chalkboard paint for a whole new look. Paint your table or chairs to match. Revive an old wooden worktop with a splash of paint after filling holes, sanding and priming. Give your refrigerator a cool look with a fresh lick of paint, too. Check the manufacturer's label, but with reasonable effort and investment your refrigerator can become the coolest feature in the room instead of one you disguise with magnets and shopping lists. Take care to unplug before you start cleaning and priming it.

FABRIC FACELIFT

Add new cushions, covers or textiles – a patterned throw, second-hand curtains, a pretty fabric blind – to give fresh zing to your things. Paint a bold design on a tired plain rug.

A STICKY SOLUTION

Sticky-backed plastic sheets are a great way of updating tired kitchen cabinets and shelves. Self-adhesive vinyl paper and contact sheets are great for renters and speedy makeovers. They come in every imaginable colour or pattern (toile, granite, brick, stone, whiteboard effect – whatever floats your boat and lifts your spirits) and can be applied to most surfaces. Temporary wallpaper and decals are as fun as they are flexible. Add tile stickers to dull tiles for a simple update.

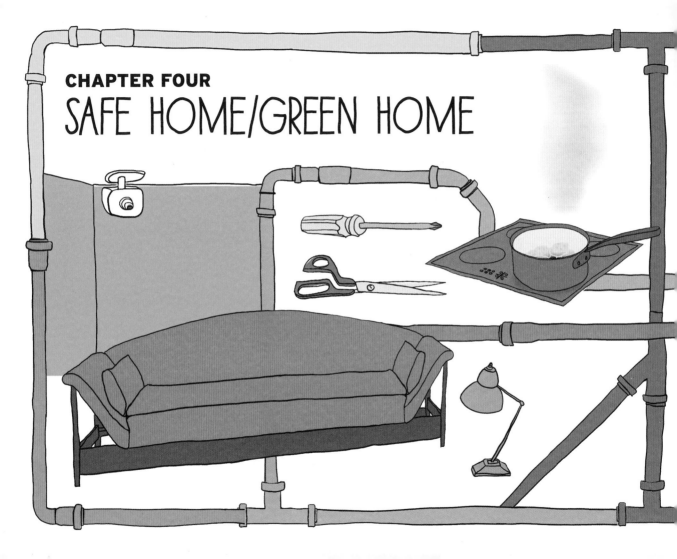

CHAPTER FOUR
SAFE HOME/GREEN HOME

LIGHTS, CAMERA, GREEN ACTION

Now you've made your home stylish and clean, it's time to focus on staying safe and being green. This chapter features useful tips on how to secure your home, keep unwanted draughts, gases, bills and burglars out and the warmth in. It will help save you money and a little bit of the planet, too.

UNDER LOCK AND KEY

Every external door needs a sturdy lock, as do windows, and even the humble letterbox is a potential weak point in your urban castle. But, as ever, help is at hand at the DIY store and there's plenty to choose from.

DON'T THROW AWAY THE KEY

If you have a conventional cylinder/night latch lock (key operated outside, twist knob on the inside), it's a good idea to fit a five-lever mortice deadlock in addition, which shoots a bolt into the door frame. Hinge bolts and key-operated rack bolts (which also shoot a bolt into the door frame) offer an extra layer of security.

Think about position too; locks should ideally be fitted away from glass that can be broken and a gloved hand inserted to undo – say – a night latch knob.

YOU'VE BEEN FRAMED

Ideally, fit locks that secure the frames together rather than those that secure just the handle. The locks for most casement windows (those attached to their frames by hinges) are fitted to the window rather than the frame, which is less secure – opt for those that are fixed to the frame. Some locks allow the option of locking while staying slightly open for ventilation.

Locks exist for most window and door types and materials, from fanlight and sash windows to those with aluminium frames, and patio doors – ask for advice.

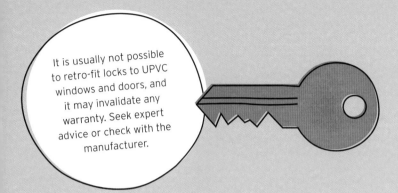

It is usually not possible to retro-fit locks to UPVC windows and doors, and it may invalidate any warranty. Seek expert advice or check with the manufacturer.

Install laminated glass in panels – it holds together even when shattered. A less expensive option is anti-shatter plastic film that is stuck to the glass; it lets in light but makes it much more difficult for thieves to smash.

MORE DOOR PROTECTION

Make use of door chains/limiters and spy holes – they're not just for little old ladies, but are also useful for checking it's the pizza delivery guy and not an energy salesman. Door limiters (like you get in hotels) are usually a bit stronger than chains, but you should ensure both are securely fitted (use the longest possible screws). A well-positioned door-chain mirror adds even more protection, allowing you to get a good look at your visitor before deciding whether to admit them.

LETTERBOX LORE

Letterboxes should be positioned at least 40cm/15¾in from the door lock to dissuade skinny burglars from chancing their arm through the slit. Nor do you want any burglars turned angler for the day, 'fishing' through your letterbox for keys and wallets left on a table. If you can't trust yourself not to leave them lying around in plain sight, fit a letterbox cage (the downside – it may clog up with mail when you are away). A brush or internal flap will hamper people attempting to peer through, though a 'fishing' implement can still be inserted.

KEEPING AN EYE ON THINGS

Invest in a security camera and spy on the dog to see how many forbidden surfaces he sprawls on in your absence. Seek advice before you buy, as there are a lot to choose from and to ensure compatibility with your devices.

BELLS BUT NO WHISTLES

Traditional 'bells-only' burglar alarm systems make a loud noise and annoy the neighbours but don't alert anyone else. More expensive systems contact a monitoring company or the police. Wired systems usually need to be fitted professionally, wireless systems use battery-powered sensors that 'talk' to a control panel and can be DIY fitted. Make sure the bell/siren box is visible – burglars who have left the dark side and gone straight say they are a deterrent, though most can spot the difference between a real and fake one used just for show.

AUTO DIALLER ALARM SYSTEMS

When triggered, the system automatically alerts you or one of your trusted people. Speech diallers operate via a landline, GSM diallers via the mobile phone network (with a SIM card). Choose a reliable phone network for your area if you opt for the latter and remember to keep the SIM topped up, or use auto top-up.

SECURITY LIGHTING

Pretending you're in by leaving one or two lights on is a tried and tested ploy. Make use of timers that turn lights on an off at certain times, as well as TVs and radios. There's no need for an Olympics opening ceremony-style light show, but make sure they are in sync, so that the TV turns off before the room light, for example. Install motion sensor lights outside front and back doors; some operate on solar power. They may flood the back door with light every time the local tomcat is out on his rounds, but they also provide security and illumination if you are fumbling for your keys in the dark.

INTERCOM SECURITY

Choose between a wired or battery-powered system that allows you to see (some have night vision) and sometimes also record visitors at the door. It can also enable you to speak to them before you decide to admit them.

BIG BROTHER

This is where Wi-Fi and smartphone technology come into their own in what is, in effect, home CCTV. You can have a single camera, or several, as part of a system, which can be wired (may be tricky to install) or wireless (may experience interference from – say – a router). Many use an app so that the camera(s) connects to your Wi-Fi network and records when movement is sensed, alerting you by smartphone or tablet. IP CCTV enables you to watch live footage over the Internet remotely

(password protect to prevent hacking).

If you have a single camera, position it in a high-traffic area (hallway, living area, etc.) that an intruder would have to cross to get to other parts of the house. Look out for the following options.

- Motion/sound detection
- One-way or two-way audio
- Video recording
- Night vision
- Siren
- Facial recognition

SOUND THE ALARMS

Alarms are all about keeping you safe and warning you of danger before it's too late. It is recommended to install at least one smoke alarm in your home (though preferably more), and carbon monoxide alarms in rooms with fuel-burning appliances. (See also Keeping An Eye On Things, pages 100–101.)

WHICH SMOKE ALARM?

Ionisation alarm Cheap, sensitive to smoke produced by fast-burning fires with flames. Slightly less sensitive to smouldering fires that give off lots of smoke pre-flames. Can be a bit trigger-happy around kitchens.

Optical/photoelectric More expensive, but less likely to have you tearing into the kitchen just because the toast is getting a little crispy. Good for smouldering fires (e.g. overheated electric wiring), slightly less sensitive to fast-burning fires with flames.

Heat alarm Sensitive to an increase in temperature above around 55°C/131°F

Some alarms can be linked so that smoke detected in one room can trigger the alarm at the others.

but doesn't detect smoke. Only covers a fairly small area, so in a large kitchen you will need several.

Combined optical/heat alarm Helps to reduce false alarms and increases the speed of fire detection.

WHICH SMOKE ALARM WHERE?

Ideally fit a suitable alarm in every room (except the bathroom, where steam may trigger it) as fire can start anywhere, but fit at least one alarm (preferably optical) on every floor of your home.

Kitchen
Just outside (not inside) Optical smoke alarm, or combined optical smoke and heat alarm.
Inside Heat alarm.

Living room, bedroom, hallway
Ideally an optical smoke alarm, or a combined smoke and heat alarm, or ionisation alarm.

Landing
Ionisation smoke alarm, or combined optical smoke and heat alarm.

Single floor (e.g. an apartment)
If you can only fit one alarm, make it an optical one between the living and sleeping areas if possible, e.g. in a hallway.

Alarms are usually fitted to the ceiling – as close to centre of the room as possible but at least 300mm/12in from a light fitting, or wall – no more than 300mm/12in below the ceiling, and away from a light fitting.

Multiple floors

One on each level, a combination of optical and ionisation alarms, linked if possible – at the bottom and top of the stairs; also in a bedroom if you have a TV in it.

OTHER FIRE SAFETY EQUIPMENT

This includes fire blankets (good for smothering cooking pan fires or wrapping around a person on fire) and domestic fire extinguishers. You can also buy escape ladders that hook over a windowsill to exit an upper floor.

Check that windows can be opened and the keys for security locks are nearby, though not in plain sight of opportunist thieves.

See also Alarm Facts and Alarms Care, page 105.

Combined smoke and carbon monoxide alarms are available, taking up less space and reducing costs.

CARBON MONOXIDE ALARM

A nasty, highly toxic gas with no odour, carbon monoxide can be produced by any appliance (e.g. a boiler, cooker, fire…) that burns gas, oil, or solid fuel (e.g. coal or wood) that is not working efficiently. Make sure you have at least one carbon monoxide alarm fitted in your home, but ideally install one in every room with a fuel-burning appliance, positioned at head height or at least 15cm/6in below the ceiling and at least 1m/39½in away from the appliance. Otherwise fit one alarm in a central location on each floor of your home and outside each sleeping area.

Telltale signs

Signs that carbon monoxide is present include sooty marks on or near gas appliances, the flame of gas appliances burning yellow/orange instead of blue, a lot of condensation in a room containing a fuel-burning appliance, and a coal or wood fire that burns abnormally slowly or goes out.

Telltale signs affecting you

These include: headache, nausea, lethargy, dizziness, breathlessness and feeling as though you have the flu. If any of these persist over time, particularly if they improve when you are away from the house, get your appliances checked. Severe carbon monoxide poisoning leads to a lessening of mental ability, loss of consciousness and eventually death. Carbon monoxide leaks are particularly deadly at night, when you are asleep and cannot take evasive action.

If your carbon monoxide alarm goes off, you risk an explosion if you create a spark that could ignite the gas.

DO NOT
- Turn on/off any electrical switches.
- Smoke, strike matches or light a flame.

BUT DO
- Get outside into the fresh air, but manually open any doors fitted with electrical security entry phones/locks.

Get suspected faulty appliances checked by a qualified professional immediately.

ALARM FACTS

- Alarms are powered by the mains or battery. Mains-powered alarms should have a battery backup in case of a power cut and have to be installed by a qualified electrician.
- Some alarms include a hush button to silence the alarm if it keeps going off when cooking, for example, or a function to temporarily silence the irritating chirp that sounds when the battery needs changing.
- Some alarms are equipped with an escape light, which is also helpful for alerting people with hearing problems, though specially designed alarms for the hard of hearing are better (e.g. a strobe light flashes or a pad below the pillow of a sleeping person vibrates).

ALARM CARE

- Test alarms regularly using the test button and vacuum the sensors to remove dust.
- Change the battery once a year (unless it's a ten-year battery). The alarm should also chirp (invariably in the middle of the night, for some reason) to let you know when the battery is on its last legs.
- It's normally best to replace the whole alarm after ten years, or as recommended by the manufacturer. Check the underside of the alarm for the date of manufacture.

DON'T LOSE IT

Saving water and energy is good for both your bank balance and the planet, so it's win-win all the way. Apart from no-brainers like switching off the light when you leave a room and fixing dripping taps, here are a other few tips for not losing it.

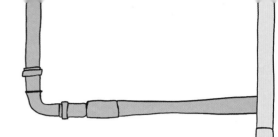

INSULATION INSPIRATION

- Look at insulating lofts (DIY or professionally) and cavity walls (professionally). Floors can also be insulated – seek professional advice.
- Pipes that run through unheated spaces – special lagging can be wrapped around the pipes like a bandage; moulded insulation tubes are also available. Tape joins to avoid gaps and insulate the bends in pipes, too. Insulation also helps prevent pipes freezing and then bursting in a thaw.
- Cold water tanks (typically in a loft) – special jackets are available to cover the sides, but not the top directly – place a wooden board over the top first, then cover with insulation. Also insulate the pipes entering the tank and the overflow. Insulating covers are also available for taps in cold areas.
- Hot water tanks – older tanks may not be insulated but you can buy special jackets for them.
- Do away with draughts – see pages 108-110.

MORE SAVING TIPS
(IN NO PARTICULAR ORDER)

- Don't leave electric appliances on standby.

- Unplug an appliance when it is fully charged.

- Leave hot food to cool before placing in the fridge.

- Close the curtains (the heavier the better) in winter to keep out a draught.

- Turn the thermostat down by 1 or 2 degrees and wear more layers.

- Dry clothes outside rather than with a tumble dryer.

- Boil only as much water as you need in a kettle.

- Cook food in a microwave rather than a conventional oven.

- Don't cover radiators or central heating thermostats with furniture or curtains.

- Fit thermostatic valves to radiators.

- Switch to LED light bulbs – they're more expensive but prices are coming down all the time, and they are more energy-efficient and can literally last for years.

- Put lids on pots and pans to reduce cooking times.

- Opinion is divided on whether it is better to leave the heating on constantly at a low level or to switch it on and off as you need it. On balance it's probably better to switch it on and off using a timer, but you could also seek expert advice.

- Place a displacement device in a toilet cistern (certain types) to reduce the amount of water used to flush.

- Rather than run the cold tap, fill a jug with water and keep it in the fridge.

- Use full loads in your washing machine (wash at 30°C/86°F) and dishwasher.

- Take a shower rather than a bath and limit showers, which can use up to 22 litres/nearly 6 gallons of water a minute.

- Shower timers (digital or like a waterproof egg timer) help you keep an eye on time spent in the shower. Shower heads that use less water are available, but check compatibility with your shower.

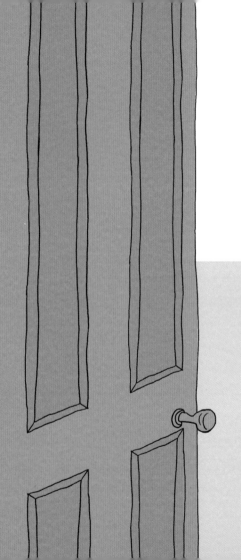

NOT GONE WITH THE WIND

Draughtproofing won't add anything to your home aesthetically, but by blocking the gaps that let warm air out and cold air in, you will be saving energy and therefore money, and will be keeping tootsies toasty in the process.

COLD FRONT APPROACHING?

Windows and doors Plug that Arctic gap with self-adhesive foam strips. A nanotechnology-free zone, they have been around for years but are cheap and effective. Check you buy the right size for the gap, cut to size, peel off the backing and stick the strip to the side of the frame the window or door closes onto. It will usually need to be replaced every few years. Internal doors that lead into a room that is not heated can be treated in the same way. Specially designed seals are available for sash windows, which can be trickier to deal with.

Base of door A metal or plastic strip with a brush or rubber skirt attached can usually be fixed to the bottom of the inside of the door with screws (can also be fixed to the top of a door). The brush version is good for uneven floors. Another option for the base of a door that is easy to fit (just slides under the door) has two polystyrene tubes

It is usually not possible to retro-fit metal or plastic strips to UPVC doors, and it may invalidate any warranty. Seek expert advice or check with the manufacturer.

on either side, but is less effective for uneven floors.

External protection for doors Also available are external draught excluder strips that are screwed into place on the door frame so that the door closes from the inside against the strip. Take care when fitting these (mitre corners) as the strips will be visible.

Letterbox Install a brush or internal flap. As an added bonus you will be making the house that little bit more secure (see page 99).

Keyhole Fit an escutcheon – a metal cover that fits over the keyhole and moves aside when the key is inserted.

Loft hatch Warm air rises, so any gaps around the loft hatch will be heating your roof space rather than your living space – use self-adhesive foam strips around the hatch frame, as for windows.

Use a junior hacksaw to cut plastic and metal strips.

SECONDARY GLAZING

Double-glazing cuts down on draughts significantly but is expensive. Secondary glazing film is an economical alternative for windows you don't need to open regularly. A thin sheet of plastic film is stuck to the window frame with double-sided tape, sealing in a layer of still air behind it. The frame has to be clean and degreased so the film sticks well. Once the film has been attached, go over the part stuck to the tape, pressing firmly to make sure the seal is secure. Then blow a warm hair dryer over the film and it will pull taut.

MIND THE GAP

Big gaps Expanding polyurethane foam sealant is a handy solution in a can – squirt it into the gap and it will expand before your very eyes. It's suitable for most materials – wood, plaster, plastic, etc. (check the manufacturer's instructions). When dry, the excess can be cut away or sanded, and you can usually paint it, too.

Gaps around pipes (such as around pipes leading to the outside/into a loft). Use a silicone filler to plug small gaps, and expanding polyurethane foam for larger ones.

Floorboards If you've gone back to nature with bare floorboards and have gaps through which an icy blast blows, fill them with flexible filler that expands and contracts with the seasons. The same applies to gaps where the skirting board meets the floor.

DRAUGHT VS VENTILATION

Don't draughtproof kitchens and bathrooms (i.e. rooms where a lot of moisture is produced), or rooms with an open fire or flue, without first checking with an expert, as these rooms need good ventilation.

Ventilation is a good thing. It is important to keep air coming in from outside to keep the air in the home fresh and to help reduce condensation – providing the air comes in through the right places – wall vents, etc.

ACKNOWLEDGEMENTS

Special thanks to Alison Parr and Ian Beattie for their very sound and sensible practical advice.

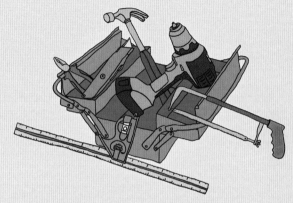

STOCKISTS

Blinds
Blinds 2Go (blinds-2go.co.uk)
Hillarys (hillarys.co.uk)
Thomas Sanderson (thomas-sanderson.co.uk)

Paint
Annie Sloan (anniesloan.com)
Crown (crownpaints.co.uk)
Dulux (dulux.co.uk)
Johnstones (johnstonespaint.com)

Paint, wallpaper, furnishings, equipment, etc.
Argos (argos.co.uk)
B&Q (diy.com)
Dunelm (dunelm.com)
Homebase (homebase.co.uk)
IKEA (ikea.com)
John Lewis (johnlewis.com)
Laura Ashley (lauraashley.com)
Tesco (tesco.com)
The Range (therange.co.uk)
Wilko (wilko.com)

Tools and equipment
Screwfix (screwfix.com)
Tool Britannia (toolbritannia.co.uk)
Tool station (toolstation.com)
Wickes (wickes.co.uk)

Vintage and salvage
English Salvage (englishsalvage.co.uk)
Love Salvage (lovesalvage.com)
Preloved (preloved.co.uk)
Secondhand Vintage and Reclaimed (secondhand-vintage-and-reclaimed.co.uk)

First published in the United Kingdom in 2017 by
Portico
43 Great Ormond Street
London
WC1N 3HZ

An imprint of Pavilion Books Company Ltd

ISBN 978-1-91023-255-2

A CIP catalogue record for this book is available from the British Library.

10 9 8 7 6 5 4 3 2 1

Reproduction by Mission Productions Ltd, Hong Kong
Printed and bound by 1010 Printing International Ltd, China

This book can be ordered direct from the publisher at www.pavilionbooks.com